The Other Side

Michael H. Brown

Happy 40th anniversary Eddy!

Mom & Dad

Spirit Daily Publishing
www.spiritdaily.com
11 Walter Place
Palm Coast, Florida 32164

The publisher recognizes and accepts that the final authority regarding the apparitions in the Catholic Church rests with the Holy See of Rome, to whose judgment we willingly submit.

—*The Publisher*

The Other Side by Michael H. Brown

Copyright © 2008 Michael H. Brown

Published by Spirit Daily Publishing

For additional copies, write:
Spirit Daily Publishing
11 Walter Place
Palm Coast, Florida 32164

or contact: www.spiritdaily.com

ISBN 9780615226750

Printed in the United States of America   First Edition

For my children

"I know a man in Christ who fourteen years ago—whether in the body I do not know, or out of the body I do not know, God knows—such a man was caught up to the third heaven. And I know how such a man—whether in the body or apart from the body I do not know, God knows—was caught up into Paradise and heard inexpressible words, which a man is not permitted to speak" [2 *Corinthinas* 12:2-4].

"Then I went through a gate that was brighter than normal daylight, into a place where the entire floor shone like gold and silver. The light was indescribable, and I can't tell you how vast it was" [Salvius, bishop and holy man in the sixth century].

"Do not quench the Spirit; do not despise prophetic utterances. But examine everything carefully; hold fast to that which is good; abstain from every form of evil" [1 *Thessalonians* 5:19-22].

1

Beyond Your Wildest Imagining

Astonishingly enough, life does not end with death. We live forever. In the light of that truth, all other things—including the most severe trials of life—pale by comparison.

There is nothing of greater importance. The more you think of it, the more astonishing it becomes.

All of us will take a last breath.

But upon that last breath, we'll rise out of our bodies, look down upon what were our physical "vehicles," and either linger for a while (perhaps to assist loved ones in their grief) or go immediately into a Light that will shortly and wondrously be described to you.

In that Light we will be met either by the Lord, angels, or deceased loved ones.

If that's not good news, I'm not sure what is.

Great news. Incomprehensible. Wondrous.

But, again, it is true: *the best news we could hope for—* the best we could expect—is an actual reality.

Upon leaving the body, which is sort of like our clothing, or spacesuit (while in this reality), we take on an entirely new existence.

A "passing" it will be: from this domain of wind and water and fire, from this dust, from this physicality, into realms of light.

New dimensions will one day unfold to you faster than could be reckoned by your computer. Your mind will out-speed the fastest chip. Knowledge—and transport—will be instant. The endless questions you have harbored your entire life will be answered in a flash by the Lord and make perfect sense. You will encounter endless secrets about your own life—amazing yourself. Existence itself will suddenly become vast. "Oh, now I see," you will think. "I never thought of it like that. Of course! I should have known. This is where I belong. Now it makes sense."

With that sudden knowing will come not only a full understanding of your entire existence, but a tremendous sense of well-being.

Now you will know that not a single thing bad ever happened to you, that what occurred was allowed by a totally loving God for your own good, that all is well, will always be well, and for the most part—no matter how it seemed—always was well if you followed Scripture.

God was always there.

Unless you are headed for a dark place, the feeling will be, "I'm home. I'm really home. This is my home!"

And that feeling will be overwhelming.

In a twinkling (and many things will be in an instant) you'll realize the truth of life and that earth is not even close to the place where you truly belong and is what the Mother Church, Catholicism, has said: It is a place of exile, of testing. You are a spiritual being having a phys-ical experience.

In light of what you will see, not even the most horrible suffering of a concentration camp, of a disease, of an acci-dent, of a broken relationship, of loneliness, of oppression, of a loved one's death, will seem like much, forgotten in the flash of eternity.

You will be bathed in goodness that comes from each blade of grass.

Never before will you have felt anything approaching that level of happiness.

Tension will be unknown. There will be total acceptance. This acceptance will cause love to flow through each person (and part of the landscape) with incredible magnification. Around and through you will be joy and love such that your most memorable anniversaries, the happiest birthdays, your most magical Christmases, the joy of childbirth, are less than what you will experience on a constant basis.

It will be beyond your wildest imagination.

The minds of the great artists of earth, the composers, the painters, the Michelangelos, have wandered here—but only for a second.

Now, it will be always.

There will be no contention.

There will be no secrets.

Everyone will know—and accept—everyone else.

Light emanates in purest form from all that resides here. You will have friends you never knew and will see everyone you knew who did not choose darkness.

The reunification with loved ones will be amazing.

You will not only encounter deceased parents but your entire line of ancestors, enough to fill a stadium. *They will cheer you.* Much of your life will turn out to be better than you expected.

This is not wishful thinking. It is not imagining. It is from real accounts.

On the other side, you will finally see how everything wove in and out of each other.

Astonishment after astonishment.

That is Heaven. There is also hell. There is purgatory. We shall discuss them. But there are the higher reaches upon which we must always focus and you will have eternities to explore them.

On the other side, one universe unfolds into another in the same way that one dimension opens into countless new ones which the mind can't fathom while it is confined by five senses.

On the other side, our senses expand into the realm of other dimensions. Streams of color far more dazzling than earthly ones will materialize before you.

It is impossible for us to grasp how realities will seem physical and non-physical at the same time.

There will be feasts (if we imagine ourselves wanting a feast), but with food that is ethereal and far surpassing any on earth and not really necessary to the "body" since there is no physicality.

Those around you will seem young—in their middle twenties, perhaps into their thirties—and at peak health. Love will be their sustenance, their oxygen.

This is also the way you will appear.

Is there atonement? There is atonement.

But the overarching point is that there is unspeakable, unimaginable, and endless joy ahead of you.

This is from consistent, irrefutable testimony. It comes from folks who have glimpsed the other side and come back with extraordinarily similar accounts whether they are Catholic, Protestant, Jewish, Muslim, Buddhist, Hindu (though this hardly implies that all such religions are equal) or agnostic.

There is a world after your physical body dies and it is one case in which there is legitimate use of words such as "wonderful" or "fantastic."

There is a world after your physical body dies, and the most important thing for you during your current life is to prepare for it.

Where "awesome" has become a cliché—where it is used now as a huge exaggeration—in the afterlife it will seem like an understatement.

2

A Vision You Could Never Imagine

When you die, you will see yourself as you *never* have. Many who've had "near death experiences" testify that they rose up, looked down, and viewed their bodies from all angles at once (when suddenly they found themselves at the ceiling of a bedroom, emergency room, or surgical unit). Some were stunned at how they had appeared! At first, you may not recognize yourself.

I knew one man who thought his body was a plaster cast and couldn't figure out why the hospital would do that: duplicate his body, which he no longer inhabited.

This initial confusion will fade when you realize (equally swiftly) that your consciousness has separated from your body like a butterfly from its cocoon and you will revel in the freedom.

The clay body you once defined as yourself will seem cumbersome.

It may seem like soiled clothes.

You will feel as if you can fly—and indeed, you will begin to move as fast as thought.

You may watch the nurses and doctors work on you, or think of loved ones and suddenly see them at bedside (or in the waiting area, out of normal view).

When you die, one of the first things that will happen—sometimes *the* first thing—is that you will move beyond the deathbed, find yourself going upward at great speed, and review your entire life—every minute—from birth and perhaps even conception.

This is important: in His mercy, God acquaints us with the fact that spirit and body are different. "If there is a natural body," said Paul (*1 Corinthians 15:44*), "be sure there is also a spiritual body."As the Blessed Mother once said (allegedly) at a famous site of apparitions, you go to Heaven *"in full conscience: that which you have now.*

"At the moment of death, you are conscious of the separation of the body and soul.

"Drawn from the earth, the body decomposes after death. It never comes back to life again. Man receives a transfigured body."

"The monk Wenlock, whose vision was narrated by St. Boniface in the eighth century, reports that his departure from the body was like the lifting of a veil," notes a scholar. From his liberated vantage point, we are told, he saw that his body was "alien to his spirit."

That is usually the first aspect: realizing that you are now in spirit.

You are a consciousness—and indeed, upon death, you will not only be fully aware, but more aware than you have ever been. Your perception will be supernaturally acute. Things will seem similar—recognizable—but different. Before moving on, you may be given the choice to stay for a short period until your body is buried (in order to help console those you leave—all the while feeling full joy amid what below is grief), or of moving into the realm of spirit.

Either way, you will be incredibly aware. You will have a vision you did not even imagine.

You may see people who are miles away.

You may *hear* them.

More important is how you will see yourself spiritually. Time and again, those who have brushed death speak of reviewing their existence. "A series of pictures, words, ideas, understanding" appeared, recalled the victim of a plane crash in Utah. "It was a scene from my life. It flashed before me with incredible rapidity, and I understood it completely and learned from it. Another scene came, and another, and another, and I was seeing my entire life, every second of it. And I didn't just understand the events; I relived them. I was that person again, doing those things to my mother, or saying those words to my father or brothers or sisters, and I knew why, for the first time, I had done them or said them. Entirety does not describe the fullness of this review. It included knowledge about myself, that all the books in the world couldn't contain. I understood every reason for everything I did in my life."

So it will be with you. Few things will amaze you as much as finally realizing why you were put on earth, why you were born to the parents to whom you were born, why you married who you married, what your purpose was, and why the major experiences of your life occurred.

Soon after you "die," in short, you will see the entirety of your earthly experience. In Europe, a seer who encounters the Blessed Mother told an interviewer that at death a soul is given the light to see its whole life, "from the moment it is breathed out of the Heart of God into its mother's womb until the moment when its freedom of choice ended at biological death."

Kindly, an angel or the Lord will take you through every event of your life. In a flash, you will see—and understand— your mother's pregnancy. You will see the way she felt, and what may have influenced you in the womb. You will see everyone she spoke with while carrying you (and hear their words). *The scenes will unfold like a three-dimensional movie*—but one in which you participate, one that shows everything at once, and one that surrounds you like a circular screen or a holograph.

Incredibly, you will hear, see, and feel every significant situation of your life from both *your* perspective and the perspective of every single person who was involved in that event. The Lord will be especially interested in what you accomplished for the sake of others (as opposed to what you did for your own ego). The little old lady who made dinner for members of her family out of nothing more than love will be treated as a conquering hero while the billionaire may be met in a way that is opposite.

That day you took time to call a bereaved friend, a hurting acquaintance, a person who was lonely, will be a day you cherish because *God* cherishes it.

You will share the joy of His angels as they take another look at it like a family movie.

Your life *is* a movie. You are a player on a stage called life. You have a prescribed number of hours, minutes, and seconds to play out a life scenario that God has designed (on average, 28,690 days). There will be a sting (*1 Corinthians 15:56*). Each person in your life walks onto your stage—and what will be important in your review is how that person felt upon exiting. Were you kind? Were you sharp? Were you patient, or too hurried for personal contact? This *sense of caring* will be high on what makes or doesn't make the review enjoyable. A joy it can be!

Also, tragic.

Those who spend a lifetime causing grief or depression will feel such for themselves (as the events from earliest childhood until the moment of death play out on that "screen" before them). "I re-experienced myself doing good things, but they were fewer and less significant than I had thought," said the crash victim. "Most of the great things I thought I had done were almost irrelevant. I had done them for myself. I had served people when it served me to do so. I had founded my charity on conditions of repayment, even if repayment was merely a stroke to my ego. Some people had been helped, however, by my small acts of kindness, a smile, a kind word, little things I had long since forgotten. I saw that people were happier because of my actions and in turn were kinder to others. I saw that I had sent out waves of goodness and hope and love when I had only meant to smile or to help in a small way. I was disappointed at how few of these incidents there were. I had not helped as many people as I thought."

Thousands upon thousands have reported this review as a prominent part of their brushes with the other side and have come back to tell us about it. You can call it a "judgment"; in some ways, it *is*. But those who've had it tell us that God was not like a judge. He was not there with a gavel in His Hand. Instead, they aver, He was the kindest and most loving force they ever felt and was simply letting them see their lives in the Light of His Truth.

There will be no way to argue with it.

It's a light that hides nothing and knows all. There's absolutely no place that the Light will not know. God forgives what we correct before we die. Terrible deeds truly repented vanish. But, as we will see, it is important to clear the slate now. "I saw myself repenting—sincerely wanting God to remove the weight and guilt of actions," goes the testimony mentioned previously. "And He had. I marveled at His sublime love and that my misdeeds could be forgiven and removed so easily."

But they must be confessed.

Fascinating it will be. We'll see the forces that influenced us to become the way we were, and how God weighs that. We'll see the turns we correctly made, and the turns we missed—opportunities we let go by. We will see the way we would have been had we taken slightly different paths, and will compare them with each other.

We'll see how it felt when we shouted at someone, when we insulted anyone, when we ridiculed (even as a youngster), at the same time that we'll feel the joy when we relive all *our moments of kindness* and every instant we loved.

When it comes to the life review—to those flashbacks—many famous people will be confused at the insignificance of what they thought had been great accomplishments.

"What did you do with the talent I gave you?" they will be asked.

"Who did you help?

"What did you do for My Plan?

"What was done out of love?

"Did you do it for Me?"

What will amaze us will be the effect of thoughts.

Here on earth, with the limitations of the senses, we think the only way we affect others is by the way we speak to them, or what we *do* to them, but when we die we'll see that thoughts are as real as words and more powerful. We die in *hyper*-consciousness. The realities expand—at the speed of light. Yet, there is no frenzy. We will not lose our "breath." We will handle it in the ease of the Spirit. That force—the Holy Spirit—will allow us to know all that we wondered about as we travel toward the Light.

Contemplate the most profound questions you have ever asked and imagine them answered just about as soon as you think of them.

The Holy Spirit of God is that fast. In Him is all knowledge. In Him is anticipation of every query. Note *Psalm* 139:4: "Even before a word is on my tongue, behold, oh Lord, You know the whole of it."

He cannot answer such questions while we are in the physical because that would compromise our "test."

We will say: oh, I see why that occurred. I see what I learned. Thank God for it! I see my mistake. I see how I learned from my mistake (even though, at the time, it seemed like I failed). Oh, *that's* why such and such person was set in my path. I should have known! *Why didn't I think of that?*

This we all will encounter—although through prayer we can greatly lessen any "disappointments." In fact, we can accomplish wonders through prayer now—such that the surprises, when they do come (and eternity is absolutely teeming with them), will not be ones of regret. However great we think God is, we will be aware of how much greater He is when we reach paradise. There will be ceaseless wonders and endless instances in which we marvel at the intricacy—and yet simplicity—of Jesus. He will delight in explaining everything to us. We will finally see how He can spend infinite time with us—answering everything we ask—and yet be doing so with countless other souls in Heaven as he also watches over all of those who are still in the physical creation, as well as other dimensions.

Everything will be imbued with the Light of God and will exude it—everything, that is, beyond purgatory.

On earth, objects depend on radiation from the sun, or artificial light, reflecting it. The way they refract or absorb the sun determines their color. On earth, there are primary colors (red, yellow, and blue; all other colors come from a mixture or concentration of those, or an absence). In Heaven, there are dozens—hundreds—of primary colors and they are perceived in different ways according to the level.

In Heaven, everything seems luminous because everything yields the light of God from within instead of reflecting it from without. We are more connected. Our thoughts are our transportation.

There are stars. There are galaxies.

"Instead of a tunnel, some people report rising suddenly into the heavens and seeing the earth and the celestial sphere as they would be seen by astronauts in space," wrote a foremost researcher in this field.

When we die, we are free from the boundaries of this world and new worlds open for us. Endless worlds. Endless "universes." Some of those who have died and returned even use the term "eternities."

In eternity, there is no past or future, and so we have been in this place before. Reincarnation is not a valid concept. The truth is in the timelessness.

There will be the swirl of energy and the feeling of being whisked through all of space and time in a vortex.

Some use the term "tunnel" but that's difficult because it is not physical.

Yet, let us call it a passage. It is how we initially move so swiftly.

"As a massive field of energy began to form in the sky directly in front of me, I heard a loud, grinding mechanical noise as the mass of energy shaped itself into a cylinder funneling upwards," wrote a Catholic man. "It seemed as if the darkness of the sky turned into liquid as the mass of energy curled like an ocean wave and formed a perfect tunnel that stretched into the heavens. As I stared into the large and imposing tunnel of energy, a shimmering, luminescent-blue field of energy began to float down the tunnel toward me. As it rapidly approached, I watched the luminescent-blue field mass into a form and begin to materialize into an image of a human being. As the image composed itself, I found myself face to face with an old friend."

Some refer to the tunnel as part of a "void": a brief trip through a dark way, unless one is bound to the earth.

"For some souls, the void is a beautiful and heavenly experience because, in the absence of all else, they are able to perfectly see the love and light they have cultivated within themselves," noted another researcher.

Some hear the sound of whooshing. Others, a buzzing, or a roar. There may be crystal-like sparks.

"The descriptions are many but the sense of what is happening remains the same: the person is going through a passageway toward an intense light," says a medical researcher I have quoted. "I have heard this space described as a cave, a well, a trough, an enclosure, a tunnel, a funnel, a vacuum, a sewer, a valley, and a cylinder."

"It started at a narrow point and became wider and wider," said another who experienced it. "But I remember it being very, very black. Even though it was black, I wasn't afraid because I knew that there was something at the other end waiting for me that was good."

Others describe going through doors, or around a hedgerow, or over a mountain—all symbolic of a passage into a new dimension.

Here we immediately relate to the passage in *Psalms* 23 that describes "the valley of the shadow of death"— and vows that no fear is needed there (if we are right with God).

A valley. A fence. A wall.

Perhaps there is a whispering. Perhaps there is a whirring. A buzz.

Angels accompany us on this journey (unless we have rejected them).

"I remember a total, peaceful, wonderful blackness," said a woman. "Very peaceful blackness."

Like total nothing but *through* something.

"It's so pleasant that you can keep going," said yet one other.

"I felt as though I was—well, that's the hard part to explain—like you're floating," testified a young man who died in a motorcycle crash. "Like you're *there* and, believe it or not, the color is—there is no color; it's darkness. It was empty. Space. Just nothing. Nothing but *something*. It's like trying to describe the end of the universe."

"Suddenly, an enormous explosion erupted beneath me, an explosion of light rolling out to the farthest limits of my vision," said a woman named Kimberly Sharp. "I was in the center of the Light. It blew away everything, including the fog.

"It reached the ends of the universe, which I could see, and doubled back on itself in endless layers. I was watching eternity unfold. The Light was brighter than hundreds of suns, but it did not hurt my eyes. I had never seen anything as luminous or as golden as this Light, and I immediately understood it was entirely composed of love, all directed at me.

"This wonderful, vibrant love was very personal, as you might describe secular love, but also sacred."

3

In Death Can Be Terrific Joy

Of course—and crucially—caution is in order. There are false "lights." There can also be a shining darkness. At a time of deception, it is important to follow the Church and Bible. Invoke the Blessed Mother. Meditate on the final words of the *Hail Mary*. Look for Jesus, and throughout life, ask your angel to be there. "If you would abandon yourself to me, you will not even feel the passage from this life to the next life," Mary has said. "You will begin to live the life of Heaven from this earth."

In the funeral liturgy: "May the angels lead you into paradise."

Beautiful was the story of a Fort Wayne, Indiana, girl named Kelleeanne Jackson who nearly drowned but was revived in the ambulance after paramedics thought they heard her last breath. "I went to Heaven," claimed the child. "I sat on Gabriel's lap. My dog that died ran to me. I saw my ancestors. I told Gabriel, 'I miss my family,' and he said he loved me, and [removed] me off his lap."

The point is that there is a whisking from one place—a physical place—to another.

The important point also is that we want to avoid a fearful (or even mildly unnerving) transition.

This is not only possible but exactly what we should spend our lives aiming for: a beautiful passage. Pray for this daily.

We can all achieve it.

Everyone reading this has time.

What it takes is viewing every moment as if it is your last.

Live every moment as if you are dying and you will be more alive than ever.

Watch fear dissipate.

That's not to say that death will be without pain, nor some anxiety. This is possible. To the final moment, there are the trials of life. Often, pain is the thing that finally purifies us.

But so merciful is God that many are those who say they left their bodies before the trauma that ended their lives— before they actually drowned, before the final moment of an accident.

"I was on a rafting trip with friends when we came upon heavy rapids," noted one account. "We tried to avoid them, but were sucked into the whirlpool. My raft capsized and I was sucked under the water for about twenty seconds, the first time.

"I popped out and was then pulled down again for about thirty seconds.

"I started to panic, fearing death by drowning. I popped out again and was thrown against a rock only to be pulled down again.

"*At that time, my spirit was out of my body* and I was watching myself struggle under the water," he continued. "At first I was afraid, but almost at the same time I felt a calm all over me. I was at the same level in the water, about six feet from my body, watching myself and two of the other people who were struggling under the water. I believe this continued for about thirty seconds until I was once again thrown against a rock. When I hit the rock for the final time, my spirit popped back into my body."

In His mercy, God often removes the terror that we usually associate with death.

"In October of 2000, I had a car accident," said another. "Although I knew I would die some day, I was in utter shock that it could be then. At that time I had absolutely no doubt that I wouldn't walk away from it. Then my mind screamed, 'I'm going to die right now!' My shock turned to absolute fear and pure horror. I have never felt such intense fear in my life. As I said, I have no visual memory as this is happening. It's as if I was in a dark void. I have no recollection of having any type of form, just thought.

"Then a calming voice communicated into my mind the thought, 'Yes, but it's okay.'

"I was immersed, engulfed by total love, totally enveloped by this Divine Presence in a way that I simply can't put into words in a fashion that anyone would understand unless they had the same experience."

To think of dying seems so morbid but not when we realize that we live forever and can forge a joyous passage.

There may be a darkness but it is not a loss of consciousness (there is no "sleep"), and for those who are in the Light of God, it will be but a flash, an instant.

Only a quarter of those who have near-death episodes report the tunnel, although we can't tell if that's because it is an actual percentage or because others forgot that part of the episode.

When we go through that passage, it is to shed our earthly countenance. It is the beginning of knowing who we really are. We may feel like we have been here before.

Are you obsessed with your house, your car, or a person? Are you overly attached to any belongings—furniture, jewelry, money in general? Do you have addictions you can't shake, especially in the way of alcoholism, sex, or drugs?

We die with our hang-ups—they literally tie us up—and with them cannot gain direct entry into Heaven.

When a young man named George Ritchie "died" in 1943, he said a deceased woman who had died with a nicotine addiction and was begging a living woman (who of course couldn't hear her) for a puff on her cigarette.

In another case, Ritchie—who was in medical school at the time (he later became a psychiatrist)—was allegedly shown a dingy bar and disembodied spirits who had died without shaking free of alcoholism and were trying to clutch at drinks.

We can't know the actual mechanics. No one has that full picture—no mystic, no theologian. But we can say that *we die as we have lived* and when we die, we do so with the same frame of mind (because mind is spirit).

If we have begun to build Heaven on earth, we take that with us.

If we refuse to follow God, if we refuse His Light, we stay stuck in a dark place with our minds attached to what had obsessed us. "I became faintly aware of other spiritual beings zipping and zinging along the tunnel with me," said a witness to the other side. "Some were going in my direction, while others headed the other way. Still other beings just stayed nearly stationary. I could sense feelings of intense bewilderment and confusion emanating from deep within their spiritual core. I had no sense of time. Time did not exist. The only thing which existed with certainty was the tunnel, me, other spiritual beings, and a very distinct pinpoint of light in the far distance. As I raced towards it, the light grew in size."

All these aspects will play out mysteriously.

"I saw that I had been on display my entire life," noted a woman. "Every thought, word, and deed of mine that I had assumed was performed in secret had been recorded since my birth and was now being fully exposed in the light of day. Everything that I ever did in secret was now brought out into the light for full review in front of God and all the Heavenly Hosts! Now, my entire life was being laid out bare before them."

What is negative in us must be removed before we are in the Presence of the Almighty.

We'll see what we contributed in the way of light. This illumination will not be from us but from Christ. I recall one woman saying that in her life review she saw how a single person being abrupt or nasty with the teller at a bank could spark a chain reaction—a reaction that could reach everywhere, that could even end up in a homicide. One person is rude to another who then is rough on a third person who has a terrible day and takes it out on everyone else, some of whom do the same, until finally a rude encounter pushes a person who is unstable to the edge.

When we smile, when we're kind, on the other hand, when we show generosity, goodness spreads like a circle of light.

Light is purity and purity is light.

God will not care about your standing in society. He will not count as good what you did for yourself. Especially, He will not care about your material things.

Instead, the Lord will startle you by showing you how things you attributed to your own talent or effort were actually gifts from *Him*. When you die, He might say something like, "I gave you a million dollars. What did you do with it to further My plan?"

"I saw a flash of a bunch of my life memories, feelings and thoughts, as well as my position as a person, more like the position of my spirit in the universe," said a man who died at seventeen from acute bronchitis. The Lord, he said, "was not disappointed with me, but in essence communicated to me that I was not fully developed in my position spiritually. I wish there were better words to describe this. He never said these exact words, rather sent these feelings to the deepest core of me. I do specifically remember feeling very immature and like I was five years old or something. The incredible peace I felt, along with this intense longing to simply be at his side, to never leave Him, to beg Him to never leave me, I felt very attached to Him. It was like the love you have for your parents but a million times."

Critical here is the word "mission": On the other side we'll see what our missions were and whether we fulfilled them.

It is very important to have fulfilled a mission at the time of death, and so we must pray to know what we need to accomplish.

Such prayers allow us to glimpse our lives from an eternal perspective.

Did you get in the way?

Even if you only have a short time to live, you can accomplish what was set out for you if you have faith and dedicate yourself (without ceasing) to the Will of God.

The person who had striven to be a CEO might have had a mission that simply was to be kind to the elderly.

Did he fulfill it?

Are you fulfilling yours?

How often and how long have you meditated upon your life mission? How much effort have you spent attempting to discern what it is and the extent of it? Have you defined what your mission should be, or has God?

All will be clear to you on the other side—not in a way that will cause you depression but rather in the way of enlightenment (God is Light, truth is Light), so that you can set out to rectify what needs to be rectified in the hereafter.

We are all sparks of God's love, and we each have a unique mission in disseminating it.

When the physical body is removed, noted a researcher, we step into the spiritual condition we have been building within us.

Upon death, the soul gravitates to the level of eternity where it fits. The greater the love, the closer we are to Heaven. Like a coin in a slot, the soul fits into its proper location. God does not choose our eternity so much as let us choose it for ourselves, and love is a ticket to the higher reaches (while coldness of heart brings the greatest danger).

"If I lived a billion years more, in my body or yours, there's not a single experience on earth that could ever be as good as being dead," said a woman who was electrocuted (but survived to tell about it).

4

How Not to Fear Death

The general rule is: hellish life, hellish afterlife; heavenly life, heavenly afterlife.

Every joy you have caused will await you in eternity.

"I not only saw it in my life review, but I relived every exact thought and attitude; even the air temperature and things that I couldn't have possibly measured when I was eight years old," said Thomas Sawyer, a Rochester, New York-area man who died when a truck he was working on feel off a jack. "I wasn't aware of how many mosquitoes were in the area. In the life review, I could have counted the mosquitoes. Everything was more accurate than could possibly be perceived in the reality of the original event."

In that review, said Sawyer, he saw all the unfulfilled desires of his life—and what would have happened if they *had* been fulfilled.

It was through "the eyes of Jesus Christ,'" said Sawyer. It was "not judgmental or negative." It was done with the "unconditional love" and total honesty of Christ.

What the Lord wanted to know from a Catholic therapist at Texas Medical Center—who "died" from an aneurism—had nothing to do with her accomplishments or degrees or accolades but whether she had exercised the love she now felt from God on the other side. "The worst thing is not being compassionate to one another," this woman, whose name is Mary Jo Rapini, told me—as did others.

At first there may be fear, but this dissolves quickly. "I was sucked into a narrow tube, and I began flying through it feet first," said the Utah woman. "The tube was extremely tight, and I became more frightened because it almost felt like my body was being sucked inside out. My speed was tremendous—indescribable. Nothing on earth has ever gone that fast; nothing could. It felt as if I were whizzing past galaxies, but the colors and lights were right next to me, almost brushing against me."

Before the endless vistas of grass on radiant hills, however, before the profusions of flowers on hillsides far beyond the gardens of earth, before the splashes of colors we have never imagined—the millions of tints, the tinges of orange that defy explanation, that make the most brilliant earthly hue seem drab, before the shades of rose and hints of pink that stretch on forever—is the purgation.

"In purgatory there are different levels," the Blessed Mother has declared at the reputed site of Medjugorje. "The lowest is close to hell and the highest gradually draws near to Heaven. It is not on All Souls Day, but at Christmas, that the greatest number of souls leave purgatory. There are in purgatory souls who pray ardently to God, but for whom no relative or friend prays on earth. God allows them to benefit from the prayers of other people. It happens that God permits them to manifest themselves in different ways to their relatives on earth in order to remind people of the existence of purgatory and to solicit their prayers to come close to God, Who is just but good."

Upon death, said one seer (in the words of an interviewer), the soul is "given the 'light' to see its whole life, from the moment it is breathed out of the Heart of God into its mother's womb until the moment when its freedom of choice is ended at biological death."

In such a light, "a soul can see the fruit of every choice and decision the soul has ever made."

At that moment, "the soul knows where it belongs."

In that assessment are not just classic "sins," but times that we had ignored responsibilities. When one person fails in his mission, all of us are hurt in some way, said RaNelle Wallace. When one succeeds, we all benefit. We were created to become partners with God in bringing goodness to the earth—to use our energies to fulfill the purposes of Christ (and to bring all brothers and sisters back to Him). Wishing everyone well is the only way to directly enter Heaven.

In the "light," said a seer from Medjugorje, in Bosnia-Hercegovina, "a soul can see the fruit of every choice and decision the soul has ever made. [The Blessed Mother] says at that moment, the soul knows where it belongs. The soul happily enters Heaven if its choices have been totally compatible with God's Will. The soul, however, gratefully accepts purgatory, a place of some sort of reparation. Here a soul must wait until someone else among the people on earth corrects, through God's graciousness, all the deliberate violations that soul has caused to God's loving Plan for the universe and to His beloved children who interacted, in His Plan, with that soul."

We'll get to more on purgatory shortly.

The tunnel pulls those in it with what seems like a speed greater than that of light. *Is it like a time warp?* Is this why it seems dark? "I was surrounded by a feeling of absolute peace and what I can only describe as unconditional love," recounted a person who drowned at seven years of age. "I was no longer able to see my body in the x-ray room," added another who died as a high school sophomore in 1988. "My world was utter darkness. I sensed myself but nothing was there. There was an indescribable feeling of love and warmth. It could be like a child before birth in its mother's womb. I felt nothing but peace and tranquility. I never wanted to leave—it was as if I was searching for this place my whole life. This place was perfection in all its aspects except that I was alone. As soon as that thought came to mind, my feeling of stillness amid the darkness instantly changed to a movement of intense speed. It was at that moment that I knew I was not alone."

Each experience is unique. Sometimes, the deceased pass others who are "traveling." There are saints. There are angels. There is communication by thought (which is prayer). There are those stuck.

"When I died, I didn't flow through a long, dark tunnel," wrote a minister named Don Piper from Texas. "I had no sense of fading away or of coming back. I never felt my body being transported into the light. I heard no voices calling to me or anything else. Simultaneous with my last recollection, a light enveloped me, with brilliance beyond earthly comprehension or description. In my next moment of awareness, I was standing in Heaven."

"I began to experience the most wonderful feelings," commented a woman who left her body after a heart attack. "I couldn't feel a thing in the world except peace, comfort, ease—just quietness. I felt that all my troubles were gone, and I thought to myself, 'Well, how quiet and peaceful, and I don't hurt at all.'"

Those who experience the tunnel say that they were moving but not really moving—that it was acceleration but more than that, and different because the legs were not working, they were not moving one after another, nor was there anything mechanical. There is acceleration toward a point of illumination. The light grows. It attracts. Can it be

Satan disguised as an angel of light? This is something one has always to bear in mind—communicating only in the Name of Jesus. Some see different colored lights, while others hear what sounds like a cylinder. It is the "speed," perhaps, that gives the sensation of a tunnel—*the way space curves around the person in spirit flowing toward God.* A massive field of energy. For some, a tornado—and here we look at the metaphor in the *Wizard of Oz.*

There is a whoosh for some, a buzzing for others, sometimes a roar, a chime for certain folks (rhythmic and in succession).

For some the passage is short. For others, a thousand miles.

It is like floating in a vacuum.

It is here, sometimes, where lost loved ones are first encountered.

"The tunnel was dark and every once in a while something looking like lightning would flash across my path," recounted a woman who had died during heart surgery at the tender age of thirteen.

Let's flash back to Salvius, a sixth-century holy man who spent a night on a funeral bier but came to when God sent him back to serve the Church as a bishop. "Four days ago, I died and was taken by two angels to the height of Heaven," he testified. "And it was just as though I rose not only from this squalid earth, but even the sun and moon, the clouds and stars. Then I went through a gate that was brighter than normal daylight, into a place where the entire floor shone like gold and silver. The light was indescribable, and I can't tell you how vast it was."

There is this complexity: the passage is a passage but for some also a meeting place, a spot of reunion, a place of grace, while for others it is a destination. Such depends, it would seem, on where the soul is headed—where it needs to go in preparation for the levels of Heaven. We can only speculate. Remarkably, the key point is that however strange it may seem, it causes no fear in those experiencing it—at least not in most cases (although there have been hellish passage experiences). In some cases, it lasts for but a blink of the eye, and then there is paradise. It is vast. It is cloud-like. It is real and yet not anything physical. It may branch into various destinations. In virtually all cases, there is the Light. It is small and yet like that "billion carbon arcs," bringing "a sense of love and camaraderie."

"I remember a very powerful force pulling me towards a serene, very beautiful realm, a higher realm," comes a testimony. "I traveled very slowly along a tunnel toward a bright light, and I could feel an overwhelming sense of warmth and peace and whiteness. I wanted to walk into the whiteness, which was so tranquil and happy. It was like stepping into a vacuum, there was nothing tangible, no scenery to look at, but a tremendous feeling of being some-where, like nirvana. I felt okay, as though this was where I was meant to be, as if I had arrived home, and I was at ease with myself for the first time in a long time."

"We began moving through space," said a woman. "I was aware of this because the stars and planets were passing very quickly. It was very exciting."

The speed at which we move is determined by our affection for the Lord. Love is the force of propulsion. Is it like the Holland Tunnel, or the eye of a hurricane? It is the route to the place of our most sacred nature. This too has been said by those who experience it: We return to our most essential "who we are."

There is energy, and the tunnel seems like a raw form of it. At any rate, the journey ends at a place that opens up to a wonderment of light. There is often a barrier. Call it the "pearly gates." Here is the landscape. There are those who encounter a valley, a river, a row of hedges, or some sort of partition which if crossed would mean permanent passage, as I have said.

There is a demarcation, the point of no return.

These are ways that the earthly mind interprets what occurs in realms it can't digest.

There are often pastures—initial expanses.

Whatever gets in the way of His Light forms the separation into which we enter.

Researchers into the phenomenon of near-death occurrences say that besides Heaven, the tunnel may lead to a "void" that is described in many ways but can be seen most readily as a place where souls are rinsed to whatever degree they need to be purified. When an atheistic Soviet doctor named George Rodonaia was hit by a car in 1976, he found himself in a realm of total darkness. The gloom was absolute, "darker than any dark, blacker than any black," says Rodonaia, and he was horrified. It was only when he turned from his negativity that the Light of God broke that awful, living darkness (awaking him as a pathologist sunk an autopsy knife into him. He is now a minister).

On the way to Heaven, pretenses dissolve and we are alone with who we really are.

Those who cultivated much love find it pleasant. Those who were obsessed or addicted may find themselves unwilling to leave this place, for they want to remain on earth to experience their obsessions. Souls that move on but need cleansing find themselves in an "in-between" gray area.

Those who are evil generally find themselves in a different circumstance. Their "tunnel" has been described as a sewer, a cylinder, or a downward spiral to a dark (or fiery) abyss.

Hell exists. One gets there by a final rejection of God. One gets there through hatred.

A man named Bill Wiese described a vision of a hellish cave in which "my gaze followed up the sides of a wall and I saw that there was a hole in the top of the cave. It was the entrance to an upward tunnel, approximately thirty-five feet in diameter. The fiendish creatures lined the tunnel walls as well. They were distinctly wicked. Their eyes were cauldrons of evil and death. Everything was filthy, stinking, rotten, and foul. There was one other distinguishing aspect about these creatures—they all seemed to possess a hatred for mankind. They were the epitome of evil. The creatures seemed to be chained, or attached in some fashion, to the cavern walls. Suddenly, I began ascending up through the tunnel. I didn't know how I was able to ascend or why. At first I rose slowly, and as I went higher, I could view the vast wasteland of hell. I could now see more of the enormous pit, which looked to be as much as a mile across. However, this was just a fraction of hell's space. To the right of the large inferno were thousands of small pits, as far as I could see. Each pit was no more than three to five feet deep – each pit holding a single lost soul. *Psalm* 94:13 refers to these pits by saying, 'until the pit is dug for the wicked.'"

The Soviet doctor who was caught in the void only broke out when he realized the existence of God.

This is crucial: acknowledging Him and doing it with love. Making a decision for love is making a decision for the Light and the power behind the Light is what propels us through the tunnel and away from any netherworld or lower purgatory.

In the famous words of one, "God is love, love is light. Light is life. God is the light of the life that loves."

When she died in the plane crash, asserted RaNelle Wallace, she was met by her grandmother, who told her that "it is within the simple principles of the Gospel that the mysteries of Heaven are found.

"We grow by the force of our desires to learn, to love, to accept things by faith that we cannot prove. Our ability to accept truth, to live by it, governs our progress in the spirit, and it determines the degree of light we possess. Nobody forces light and truth upon us, and nobody takes it away unless we let them.

"The scene was sacred beyond words, beyond expression, and those who have witnessed it keep it hidden in their hearts. I saw that I had indeed lacked faith, that love isn't simply a word or an emotion; love is a power that gives action to all around it. *Love is the power of life.*"

And the afterlife.

We go through the tunnel toward the light with a speed *in proportion to how much we have loved.* We do not get there through theology (though this has its place). We get to the light through what is in the deepest recesses of *who we are,* and who we are is quickly revealed in the transition.

No falsity can move forward.

Joy is the greatest barometer of whether we are living right. We create joy and then *step into it.*

Or we do the opposite.

It is not hard to avoid an unpleasant afterlife.

"At the evening of life," said St. John of the Cross, "we shall be judged on our love."

"It is a life of love, a life of behaving honestly and fairly in every task, that leads to a heavenly life," said a philosopher who had glimpses of the beyond.

Do not be a slave to earth and you will not be enslaved to it.

In those cases where no "tunnel" is encountered, the transportation is instant but will also include a review of what we have done.

Those who die and return had more work to do.

"I was 24, a registered nurse, living and working in Los Angeles County," said Eileen M. Carol from Santa Rosa,

California, who clinically died on April 3, 1965, in another plane accident. "My boyfriend was 26 and an engineer at McDonnell-Douglas, and almost every Sunday afternoon we would go flying in his two-seater Luscombe-A airplane out of Long Beach, California.

"This was the only day in my life I had a premonition not to go. But, I never acted on it, as I did not want to appear fearful of flying. It was a beautiful sunny April afternoon in southern California. Because it had been so dry and warm, rangers were stationed in the fire towers in the Cleveland National Forest in the mountains.

"We had friends who were house-sitting at a ranch at the end of Black Star Canyon in the Santa Ana Mountains and they mentioned that there was an air strip there. We wanted to fly over and check it out for a possible future visit. We waited an unusually long time to take off from Long Beach Airport. Single-engine airplanes have to wait for jets, twin-engine and higher priority airplanes to land and take off.

"We waited for over twenty minutes before we were cleared for take-off. It was just after 3:00 p.m.

"We were flying parallel to the Santa Ana Mountains," continued Eileen. "Our plan was to fly along and count the canyons. When we arrived at Black Star Canyon we would turn into the mountains and follow the road until we got to the top to sight the ranch and runway. We were following flight regulations—a thousand feet above the terrain—and while my boyfriend was flying, I was navigating from maps.

"As we neared our destination—the last canyon on the map—I told my boyfriend to make a full circle to the right so we could check out our bearings. I wanted to make sure we would be turning to follow the correct canyon. I was sure we were at Silverado Canyon, which is one canyon before Black Star Canyon.

"As he turned the airplane to the right, I heard him say that he could not keep the nose of the airplane up. As he was starting the turn, I recall seeing clear blue skies and no clouds."

It was then that they crashed.

"The next thing I recall is looking out of the front window of the airplane and seeing the sun shining on rocks —I could not tell you if they were boulders or gravel," said Eileen. "My next recollection was that I was out of my body looking down on the crash scene.

"I could see the nose of the airplane in a very large shrub and it was crumpled to the right.

"There was gasoline all over the ground. The gasoline tank on the Luscombe is situated right above the passengers and it had broken open on the impact. We discovered later that we had been caught in a downdraft and pulled into a little valley in the top of the mountains.

"I was protected by a coat I was wearing, but my boyfriend had chemical burns on his torso from the high-octane airplane fuel. No electrical equipment could be used to get us out of the airplane, so saws and axes had to be used. It took them forty-five minutes to cut us out of the airplane with hand tools. There were five individuals outside the airplane. I could see them drag me from the passenger side of the airplane. I saw that my body was bloody—that my right leg was broken and that my left foot almost had been severed from my leg. I was full of joy in my spirit and was confused as to why I was feeling that way when my body was so traumatized!

"The next thing I remembered was a powerful male voice say to me. *'It is not time yet. You have work to do.'* I couldn't tell you if it was the voice of Jesus or God the Father. But I knew it was the Voice of 'God.'

"*Immediately following this*, my spirit went back into my body on the ground. I then experienced pain and recalled every thing that happened after that. We were taken to Orange County Hospital which is now University of California, Irvine. A Catholic priest was called and gave me last rites. He later married us and baptized our daughter. To this day I have never feared death. I have never really known what my 'work to do' meant. Was it my nursing? Or, is it my present ministry of being a prayer warrior? Participating on prayer teams? Praying with my patients (I am a family nurse practitioner) and other people? Or, a combination of all of these?"

As we will see, such is a common experience.

"You have work to do."

One isn't quite ready to die.

But we note how even the most terrifying "death" can pass joyously, through God and His mercy, when we are not hellbound.

In fact, said Dr. Ritchie, death is "simply a door we walk through."

"Don't worry," a young girl who "drowned" told a medical researcher. "Heaven is fun!"

5

Your Transition to the Other Side
Is Personal

And so we see to this point that death is a transition that is similar and yet different for everyone and is in the full control of Christ.

"I wasn't sure when the light in the room began to change," said Dr. Ritchie, who encountered the luminosity when he simply found himself out of his body and in that hospital standing next to his bed. "Suddenly I was aware that it was brighter, a lot brighter, than it had been. I stared in astonishment as the brightness increased, coming from nowhere, seeming to shine everywhere at once.

"All the light bulbs in the ward couldn't give off that much light. All the bulbs in the world couldn't! It was impossibly bright . . .

"I saw that it was not light but a Man who had entered the room, or rather, a Man made out of light, though this seemed no more possible to my mind than the incredible intensity of brightness that made up His form. The instant I perceived Him, a command formed itself in my mind. 'Stand up!' The words came from inside me, yet they had an authority my mere thoughts had never had. I got to my feet, and as I did came to the stupendous certainty: 'You are in

the presence of *the* Son of God.' Again, the concept seemed to form itself inside me, but not as thought or speculation. It was a kind of knowing, immediate and complete."

If not Jesus, it may be an angel, or relatives—or purgatorial souls we have helped (St. Margaret of Cortona spoke of such). This meeting can happen before death, in the tunnel, or in the brightness. During the early 1900s there were studies on deathbed visions with doctors and nurses buttressing the claims of patients who said that as death approached, they saw relatives and friends who had predeceased them. God often eases us toward the other side—makes it less and less frightening until those facing it look forward to it, having seen dead husbands or parents and now ready to join them.

It is often the relatives who tell those near death that it is not yet their time, that they must "go back."

One researcher found that of the ten percent of dying people who are conscious shortly before their deaths, more than half experience such visions.

It is important to know that in the transition can be deceiving voices. That is why we invoke the saints and especially Mary to be with us. Here too is the comfort of St. Joseph.

Those prayers draw protection.

They make the passage wonderful.

Through our lives, the deceased often send us signs. Although we must be extremely cautious not to initiate such communication (which the Bible condemns as necromancy), nearly everyone has accounts of objects or photographs showing up at odd times or in odd places. An object associated with the deceased appears at a poignant moment. A song comes on the radio. A certain flower blooms at a peculiar time—a flower associated with that loved one. One woman said that she received lovely rose blooms in some fashion every year on the anniversary of her daughter's death.

"My husband, Gene, was afraid of dying, and he always asked me how I could not be afraid," a woman named Rose Best from Barstow, California, wrote me. "When he had lung cancer, he told me he was afraid. He had one chemo treatment on Dec 30, 1997. On Jan 10, 1998, he took a turn for the worst, went into respiratory distress, and I called an ambulance to take him to the hospital.

"When he was stable he was sent to a veteran's hospital, so he could continue treatment. While he was there for a few days, he called me and said he needed to talk to me, he was so confused. I told him I would be there in an hour, and I was on my way.

"When I got there he told me that he had just had an experience and wanted to tell me about it, when he had called me.

"He said he started to hear beautiful music and everything was so peaceful; he saw a bright light and he started going towards it again; he could not get over the peacefulness of where he was.

"As he was walking towards the light he was not as old as he was now—65—but much, much younger and had a spring to his step. And then he heard a voice saying it was not his time and calling him back.

"*But he said he did not want to go back*—it was a beautiful place to be; again it was said it was not his time. From that time on he prayed more and had a certain peace about him. He died a beautiful peaceful death about two weeks later. He had the Last Rites and was ready to meet his God."

"When I was told I was going to have to go back, I screamed, 'Oh no, please don't send me back. I want to stay with you,'" recounted a Florida woman—angry that she had to return.

While many near-deathers see eternity as something that transcends any organized religion—and that the most important preparation for death, by far, is love—those who belonged to a religion before they died by and large remain active in their religions when they return.

The oldest Christian faith—the Catholic one—teaches many attributes that are stressed by those who die and come back. It is a route of safe passage.

But through it all must come the virtue of love, selflessness, and forgiveness.

Through the sacraments, congregants are allowed a taste of Heaven. Heaven is *constant Communion.* The Host, as Body and Blood, is a portal—our contact with Jesus before we see Him in His Light.

But the sacraments are meant to help purify the soul, instill selflessness, and prepare for the eternal.

If not, they lose their potential.

"I know, it is an old cliché: love makes the world go round," a Kansas woman told a writer. "But you know, that is true. *I learned during my experience that it is God's Love that makes the world go round,* and the more we lend our hand to God by loving others—as well as ourselves—the more we grow spiritually."

As one person was asked: what have you done to benefit the human race?

It doesn't mean we all have to be great inventors. It doesn't mean we should all lead a nation.

It means we must exhibit kindness and fulfill our particular duties, which were assigned in the Mind of God before the beginning of the world.

If those duties are not fulfilled, we are sent back.

We are sent into the world for a purpose and do well always to pray that the mission is fulfilled.

Can we accept those who assert they can even remember brushes with death that occurred *in the womb*?

"My story begins before my birth," a housewife named Lin Mongan of Kaukauna, Wisconsin, told me. "Near full term in her pregnancy, my mother was losing me in the womb. The doctor informed her that the cord was wrapped around my neck, and I was fighting for my life. I was aware of everything going on before the doctor arrived due to the fact that I was hovering over my mother in spirit. I recall trying to appeal to her—that I must survive! I remember knowing she was my earthly mother, chosen for me by Our Lord God. I recall a near panic, in my quest to live, and repeating over and over that I had a purpose to fulfill given to me by my heavenly Father. I watched as the doctor sat with my mother, unable to do anything other than quiet her, keep her still, and wait to see if I would make it. I recall re-entry into my physical body with much pain and almost a warrior approach fighting to be able to live."

We fight to accomplish our missions, and when it is not our time, it is not our time.

Our angels are with us through life and during the transition (aiding us too in purgatory, if that's where we go).

In Florida, two strangers saved a two-year-old from drowning, and then disappeared.

When it is not our time, the Lord can use all His agencies.

In Charleston, West Virginia, 59-year-old Val Thomas had no pulse or brainwave activity intermittently for more than seventeen hours (her toes curled back in *rigor mortis*) yet was brought back minutes after they removed the ventilator for whatever purpose in God's mysterious designs.

Astonishing it is when two people who know each other "die" at the same moment—or around the same moment—and meet up, in the spirit, as occurred with a woman named Eloise Weaver of Utah.

Here again we see the interaction of "strangers."

Eloise, her husband, Dave, and a daughter were traveling to Montana when they were involved in a horrible accident. A car smashed into them, pinning them in their seats. But before dying, Eloise saw two mysterious people clad in tremendous white in the car window, telling her to pull her knees up to her chest, breathe shallowly, and she would then survive, which she did. But not before leaving her body.

"The paramedics got my daughter out first," she recounted to a researcher named Arvin Gibson. "Then they began to pry on the door where my husband was. Dave kept saying how badly he hurt, and they were afraid he was dying. He turned to me, and that's when everything in the car got really bright, very warm and very quiet.

"I didn't hear my daughter screaming anymore, and I didn't hear any voices coming from outside the car.

"I felt Dave's presence very close to me, and suddenly we were above our bodies. He held me really tight, and he said: 'Hang in there babe; I love you.' That's what he always called me. Then he said, 'I'm being called home, and you need to go back and raise our girls.'"

In other cases, those who die at the same time at different places have met up in that zone—that void—which separates realities.

One man near death with heart problems suddenly found himself talking with his sister—who was in another part of the same hospital *in a diabetic coma.*

They were up in a corner of the room watching the doctors work on him when suddenly she began to move away.

Recounted this man to the key near-death researcher, Dr. Raymond Moody, "I tried to go with her but she kept telling me to stay where I was. 'It's not your time.' 'You can't go because it's not your time.'

40

"Then she just began to recede off into the distance through a tunnel while I was left there alone.

"When I awoke, I told the doctors that my sister had died. He denied it, but at my insistence, he had a nurse check on it. She had in fact died—just as I knew she did."

Relatives are important both here and in the hereafter.

There is the grandfather, robed in white. There are parents. Sometimes, there are whole families. "In the distance by the river there were six or seven people standing by some trees, and I could tell that they were waiting for me," said a woman named Elane Durham.

"It was as if they knew I was coming. One of them looked up and said: 'There she is!' A man leaning against a tree motioned with his arm and said: 'Hurry, everyone's waiting.'

"Two women broke away from the group and began running toward me," continued Elane. "When they got within about twenty feet, I recognized one as my grandmother. She had been dead since I was about nine years old. The man against the tree was my mother's step-dad, and he had been dead since I was sixteen or seventeen. The lady immediately behind my grandmother was Aunt Virginia, my husband's aunt, who died the previous February."

Sometimes they are seen in the hospital room. Sometimes they are seen in the tunnel—or in the Light at the end of the tunnel. Sometimes they are on a landscape that looks like Heaven. I know a woman with spiritual gifts from Phoenix who had a vivid dream of seeing her deceased husband resting on an overlook before the indescribable rolling countryside that announces an entirely different world. "You'll be here some day," he told his beloved wife, adding, though, that she was not allowed to come closer.

"I remember being taken down to the operating theatre, and then the anesthetic worked and I was asleep," said an

English woman. "But suddenly I came back. I could see myself on the operating table with doctors and nurses rushing around me. I was up on the ceiling, looking down at my body. I didn't appear to have a body up there; I was transparent, but it was definitely the real me and I was aware of having a shape. The body that was on the operating table was somehow connected to me. I knew it was me, but it was not the important 'me' that was up on the ceiling. I could hear a nurse shouting my name, and she was holding something that looked like a rugby ball against my face—it was presumably a mask for me to breathe through. As I was watching them all panic I felt very calm and unworried. I looked sideways, towards a very bright light, and I could see an avenue of trees with green fields on either side."

While skeptics have tried to explain it as subconscious perception, that is more difficult to claim when the person who "died" can describe not only what was transpiring in the room where his body was *but also in the waiting room or even among family members many miles away* at home. There are blind people who have been able to describe the features of doctors and nurses they watched from "above." In one case, a woman was able to recall a sneaker on the roof of the hospital far out of her view—claiming she had seen it when her body rose above the building: a sneaker that was not visible from her floor, nor from the ground, but only from a certain room on the other side of the hospital.

"It was easy to give up and be quiet, easy to surrender," said Kimberly Sharp, who now researches such experiences. "I knew I was not alone, but I still couldn't see clearly, because I was enveloped in a dense, dark gray fog—not a cold fog but a warm one. I felt a sense of expectancy, the same anticipation one feels waiting for a plane to take off or arrive. It seemed natural and right to be here, and for me to wait as long as it took. Earthly time had no meaning anymore. There was no concept of 'before' or 'after.'"

"My perspective on death has changed," said Eloise. "I used to be a real coward about death. I think the fear that was in me—and that which is shared by many people—is in part because our bodies have a survival instinct; they don't want to give up. I now feel that death is a piece of cake. It doesn't scare me anymore."

6

When There Is Darkness

That's not to deny the existence of parts of the afterlife that are frightening.

These exist, and we will discuss them.

But fear does nothing. As RaNelle learned, it kept her back. In the afterlife, it blocked her powers of traveling, understanding, and progression (she relates in her book, *The Burning Within*). It was crucial—her grandmother told her—to "let go."

The time is now in your life to get rid of a fear that otherwise will last into "forever."

When she let go, secrets of existence were revealed to RaNelle in this place where "the whole garden was singing. The flowers, grass, trees, and other plants filled this place with glorious tones and rhythms and melodies; yet I didn't hear the music itself. I could feel it somehow on a level beyond my hearing. As my grandmother and I stopped a moment to marvel at this magnificent scene, I said to myself, 'Everything here seems to be singing,' which was woefully inadequate to describe what I felt. We simply don't have language that adequately communicates the beauty of that world."

It takes letting go. It takes a single word:
"Jesus."

In case after case, in brushes with death, is the encounter with Christ in a form that no one who has reported it came close to imagining.

There are many variances but there is often the early—and sometimes even immediate—appearance of Him.

He might be *in* the distance at first—immersed in Light—or He may step right into the view of whoever it is making the passage.

He may arrive like a light in the distance, a glowing comet; other times His Presence is instantaneous.

He may be in the tunnel. Usually He is the Light at the end of it.

No matter how He comes, it is with a love beyond any we could know on earth—vastly more even than that of a bride or groom on the big day, more than a mother as she glances for the first time at her baby.

Nothing on earth prepares a person for the love that Jesus exhibits, and this is recounted in so many experiences that sometimes it seems like those who *don't* recall such an encounter are a rarity.

I spoke with a woman named Linnie Smith of New Hudson, Michigan, who in 1994 was in deep distress due to a gall bladder so full of stones it was shredding her innards. For years Linnie had suffered and for years was told it was simply a problem with acid reflux. Her doctors kept sending her home, for reasons that seemed mysterious.

That December, the 43-year-old woman found herself doubled over from pain and yet still turned away by the doctor who examined her.

Linnie was frustrated, at the end of her rope, and with no recourse but Pentecostal prayer (this was before she converted to Catholicism). "I knew I was dying, that I couldn't do any more to keep 'me' in there," she related. "All I had was my faith. As I was lying there in my room, I began to tell the Lord how much I loved Him, how very much I loved Him—and when that happened the room suddenly filled with the sounds of music, bells, birds, voices, and instruments. It was the most beautiful music I ever heard. It was so harmonic. I know now why churches have bells!

"*As that music filled my room*, a foggy mist rolled in, and as it did I got farther and farther from myself. And in the blink of an eye, I was in a closed-like tunnel—but not dark. The end was not far away and it was bathed like everyone says—in a light brighter than the sun but with no yellow: pure white light, radiating out, transparent and translucent at the same time.

"It was a cloud-like tunnel revolving clockwise around me. There are no earthly words for it because you can't find it on earth.

"As a kid I used to go outside and want a cloud to come down so I could ride it and now I thought, 'Yes, I got my cloud!' That's how He cares about us. He remembered it.

"Light hit the side of the tunnel and burst into pastel colors that were *alive* and sparkling. They were so full of life, if they could have giggled, they would have. Everything there was full of life. Something drew my eyes to the light at the end of the tunnel and there was Christ. He was full of light and His Hands were out to receive me. He *was* light. There were all these shades of lighter white in His Light but with no dark—more like a prism: different shades but no darkness! It became whiter than white. An artist couldn't portray this. There was so much light coming out of Him that you couldn't see Him. His Arms were outstretched and I knew I was home and I was ecstatic!"

"Ecstasy" is the operative word.

"When I first saw Him, the light and the glory and the surging of power was so tremendous," adds a woman named Margaret Tweddell. "It was like an avalanche of feeling over me. At the present time I just don't feel that I have found a way in which to describe what it was like—an indescribable contentment and uplifting, a tremendous ecstasy of feeling on all realms, being completely out of myself, an unusually vivid knowledge of the intense, sympathetic love around you—the warmth of it, the light of it—something that's not external but is *part of you*."

It usually starts as that small speck of light. Soon, it consumes everything. There are no more tunnels. "It is like a sunrise on a mountain that is covered with snow, when the colors come down and reflect on you—a dazzling brilliance that would make you close your eyes and yet feel it in every pore of your body," said another. Again, this is part of the initial stage—usually. It can occur even in the hospital room. In addition to Jesus are His angels. We are reminded by writer Susan Tassone that "they are a most potent help for us at the hour of our death, strengthening us against temptation, and comforting us in our agony. They conduct our souls to judgment. We are assured the angels console us if we are in purgatory, encourage us, and render a most valuable service to the souls in purgatory by inspiring friends and relatives to offer Mass for their intentions and good works for speedy delivery. These devoted guardians—to whom we should pray each day (asking their help in purifying here on earth) —never cease to be concerned with the souls that God has committed to their charge. Their great mission and desire is to see us home in Heaven."

There are also the saints. There are those we have helped. There are those for whom we have prayed. When an angel appeared to Linnie Smith, it was at first as "liquid light" that poured into the room and took the form of head and wings with glorious colors—so radiant that with phys-ical eyes it would be blinding. "Angels rarely appear in their glory," recalled art professor Dr. Howard Storm, who died on June 1, 1985. "The times that angels have appeared to me in their full glory it was almost unbearable. The brightness of the light that radiates from them is brighter than the light from a welding torch.

"Their light doesn't burn the eye, but it is frightening because it is so different from our experience of life. An experience of the supernatural glory and power of an angel is frightening. They don't appear to us in their natural state very often. They most often tone it down for us to keep us comfortable. I don't have the words adequately to describe angels in their natural state. Brighter than lightning, beau-tiful beyond comparison, powerful, loving, and gentle are words that fail to describe them. The artists' depictions of angels are pitifully inadequate. As an artist I am aware of the impossibility of representing an angel. How do you paint something that is more radiant than substance? How do you paint colors that you have never seen before or since? How do you describe love on a canvas?"

For at least a moment, there is no scenery. There is only brilliance. It finally gives correct use to the term "awesome."

Yet so much brighter—and more loving—is Christ.

He is whiter than white and with that Light He searches us, wants to know the love we have, measures our charity, and desires us to act in those "small" ways that demonstrate concern for others and unselfishness.

This is key. We must lose "self." We must do that over and again. *Even little bits of pride are blocks.* Everything must be looked at as service. When we approach each major matter in life with service in mind we lose fear of death because we are demonstrating love and we are prepared for the afterlife and the inner spirit knows it. To say "I love you" must be backed by actions.

The culture of ego and profit knows no reward in Heaven. To get what one can out of another person is wrong and will be replayed for us. The modern way is the way of purgatory.

There are higher states of spirit and lower states and though the New Age has hijacked the term, it can be understood that in the realm of energy we vibrate—that our loftiest instincts cause us to reverberate at a higher, whiter level while base instincts cause us to vibrate more slowly and settle to a lower place, where there is the gray or black of purification. A low vibration of self-centeredness can get us caught in the "tunnel." Without preparation, there are dangers in the afterlife. On earth, in hell, and in the realm between—on the way to eternity—can be spiritual mischief from which purity guards us. The condemned are in a misery they have customized for themselves and we can be protected from their attempts to keep us down by simply invoking Christ. *Jesus, Jesus, Jesus.* We find ourselves in darkness and vulnerable to the degree that there is darkness—the absence of love—in our lives. The core of our beings is all that we possess upon death and that core must be filled with the light of love to get to the Light that *is* Love. If we're selfish we encounter others who are selfish—in the shadowy areas. That may be what the Bible describes as the "outer darkness" (*Matthew* 8:12). At Medjugorje a seer named Marija called it a "very misty" place with "a lot of voices begging for our prayers."

"At first it just seemed like a foggy grayness about me," said a woman named Grace Bubulka. "As the speed of my upward and outward movement increased, the enclosing fog seemed to have a bright ending at the distance."

"All around me was a gray, cloud-like, thick fog," said yet another, Chris Taylor. "The closer I approached the light the more I became aware of a fundamental sense of purity."

There are angels in the transition and, at times, also the wrong kind of angels. At the foggy periphery can be souls that seem "stuck," or entities that bear non-human characteristics. The tunnel often seems like God's way of bringing us from earth without contact with those who are in those lower regions. We shed the superficial nature. As during a crisis, the core of our true being comes out. For some the tunnel is daunting and even cold while for others it is the essence of warmth and for most it is not unpleasant—indicating that like other aspects of the hereafter it integrates a number of purposes.

It is a chamber in which we totally become our inner nature.

The only way of presenting ourselves will now be in the truth of His Light, and those who cannot face that are those who gravitate toward darkness.

Some have that feeling of traveling through space, and interesting it is that photographs taken by astronomers show nebulae or star clusters that appear to have "faces" in them (as if something spiritual is inflecting itself).

Is space simply a manifestation?

Is it like moving from one subatomic level to another?

There are universes within universes traversed at the speed of thought. These will unfold to you.

The farther we go, the more we act like who we really are. Only the best in us is allowed in Heaven and we can't go there until all we are is that best part. Then, we reach Heaven in the joy of a fantastic homecoming—a jovial reunion, an unimaginable relief in seeing loved ones, a blessed entry. In the tunnel, familiar figures are often first glimpsed at the fringes or suddenly appear to guide us through. We choose the dark—and shrug off help—when we want to continue hiding something—when we remain attached to the earth and fearful of transparency. Pride declares the truth as an insult.

If we are not transparent, if we are not willing to let ourselves be seen in our entirety, if we're embarrassed to reveal who we are, we will try to hide something, and this will inhibit us. To be transparent is to love, which is also to see the best in everyone.

If we gravitate to the lower reaches, this can mean purgatory or that earthbound state. We linger, afraid of the light, or obsessed. St. Padre Pio said he saw more deceased souls than living ones. Bad habits and addictions—over-attachment—must be shed. They are darkness. And darkness goes to darkness. It stays with the earth. A soul finds itself roaming among those who are still alive, half in the physical world, half in a spiritual one. So it is that we hear (too frequently, for outright dismissal) accounts of "ghosts." In a book called *Return from Tomorrow*, Dr. Ritchie claimed he was taken to a place where he saw a group of assembly-line workers gathered around a coffee canteen.

"One of the women asked another for a cigarette, begged her in fact, as though she wanted it more than anything in the world," he wrote. "But the other one, chatting with her friends, ignored her. She took a pack of cigarettes from her coveralls, and without ever offering it to the woman who reached for it so eagerly, took one out and lit it. Fast as a striking snake the woman who had been refused snatched at the lighted cigarette in the other one's mouth. Again she grabbed at it, and again. With a little chill of recognition I saw that she was unable to grip it."

Ritchie also saw alcoholic spirits attempting to grab drinks from drunken sailors whose own spirits were vulnerable—with a "hole" of entry—due to intoxication. Think of the very word "spirits."

That such exists is confirmed by the Bible's warning against conjuring the dead.

The dead do not pass if they refuse the Light (and remain in their addictions). Or they do their purgatory here.

"For me there was no blaze of radiance, no arms waiting to usher me into the Divine Presence," said Angie Fenimore, a woman who as a young mother took a drug overdose to commit suicide—which also leads to the netherworld. "There was only blackness, as though I were suspended in outer space, unbroken by a single glimmering star.

"Where was I? I was immersed in darkness. My eyes seemed to adjust, and I could see clearly even though there was no light. I was aware that I was standing on what felt like solid ground, but nothing was there. The darkness continued in all directions and seemed to have no end, but it wasn't just blackness, it was an endless void, an absence of light. I knew that it had its own life and purpose. It was completely enveloping.

"Death was quite an adventure. I swung my head around to explore the thick blackness and saw, to my right, standing shoulder to shoulder, a handful of others. They were teenagers. 'Oh, we must be the suicides.'

"Then came a *whoosh!* Suddenly, as if we had been waiting for a kind of sorting process to take place, I was sucked further into the darkness by an unseen and unde-fined power—leaving the teenagers behind. I was flying upright, moving at warp speed, like a comet shooting out of nowhere. I sensed that I was going faster than any man-made aircraft could fly, but without the physical effects of flight or the pull of gravity. Nor did I have any sense of the tempera-ture, of the coldness you'd expect to find in deep space, or any way to judge time. I was probably flying for a fraction of a second."

Angie found herself on the edge of a shadowy plane and shrouded in a black mist that swirled around her feet, holding her captive. Darkness had life.

"The place was charged with a crackling energy that sparked me into hyper-alertness, a state of hair-trigger sensitivity," she wrote (in a book called *Beyond the Darkness*). "The foglike mist had mass—it seemed to be formed of molecules of intense darkness—and it could be handled and shaped. It had life, this darkness, some kind of intelligence that was purely negative, even evil."

It was lowest purgatory, she was given to understand (though she was non-Catholic). I remember the dungeon of an old fort that was haunted, and every city has its stories.

We can sense the deceased because we are granted that instinct. Suddenly, they may just seem to be near us.

It does not always or even usually indicate they are earthbound. It may be God allowing them to communicate something to us—perhaps to warn, or to comfort us, or to ask for our prayers.

The same occurs in dreams.

During sleep, spirits roam and often bring back snatches of eternity.

Constant dreams about a loved one may mean that the person needs a Mass dedicated to him.

They may leave us signs such as old items that suddenly appear in a corner of a drawer at a meaningful moment or even a subtle image etched into an item in our reality. As I mentioned, at the moment we're thinking of a loved one, we may come upon a photo of that person, or an article of jewelry. It may be a simple comfort sent to us. In other cases, it occurs because a soul is overly attached to the item. Strange things have been reported in museums, with antiques, and among Egyptian artifacts. Objects can draw the energy of those who—from the other side—are obsessed with them.

This reportedly happened with a grandfather's clock in the Nevada governor's mansion. Many are the accounts of "hauntings." When there are disruptions in our homes, or sudden problems, we must consider the possibility of a departed, troubled soul. Of course, it can also be a demon.

"In 1993, when we were in our mid-twenties, my husband and I bought a beautiful 300-year-old antique home in Newburyport (a community nationally esteemed for its First and Second Period architecture)," a woman named Pamela Smith wrote me from Massachusetts. "This home had been painstakingly restored and 95 percent of its original timber, woodwork, hardware, original plaster walls, and ceilings had been preserved. What was not original had been reproduced exactly using 18th-century hand tools. The home had never had plumbing until the 1980s. When we bought it, the dining room still had not been electrified. The front Georgian entryway alone won a Congressional award for its restoration. It is a registered national landmark and has been featured in many books, calendars, and note cards, and has been painted by famous artists.

"The home's inhabitants were equally impressive. It is the quintessential Georgian sea captain's home. The chain of title to this home reads like a 'Who's Who' of Revolutionary maritime history. Almost every impressive ship owner or Revolutionary ship captain in the area owned or lived in this home. One sea captain was lost at sea while owning it. It even has one of the 'haunted,' secret tunnels of Newburyport in the basement that leads all the way down to the waterfront—used for smuggling. Someone wisely bricked the entrance closed at some point.

"Anyway, we were in love with the house, of course, and got it for a 'deal' (because of a real-estate recession) and immediately began buying beautiful antiques and settling in for what should have been a great life.

"However, behind the beautiful façade and landscaping, this home was beset with tangible, negative forces: cold, dead pockets of air in rooms that people never wanted to be in, and 'presences' that could be felt walking around the house. Even the dog would bark and growl and follow the presences throughout the house.

"When these dark beings (and that is exactly what they 'felt' like to us) would walk beneath a smoke alarm, the smoke alarm would go off until the presence had passed by. Not all the alarms would go off at once throughout the house, as they should have; they would go off individually as the presence passed by. When the children were quite small they would be standing up in their crib and 'watching' things move around their bedrooms. Original, heavy iron latches on doors would move and the doors would swing open. Balls of light would float around the original, huge walk-in cooking fireplace. 'Something' that 'lived' in the wine cellar angrily told my husband to 'Get out!' one day. Throughout the time we owned the home, flashes of light would go off constantly at night, every night, in our bedroom. It was impressive and possessed solid walls of original raised wood paneling with the doors 'cut' out of the paneling and original hardware and fireplace. It would have been used for meetings as well as a bedroom.

"We would be woken out of our sleep by the sounds of boxes being moved across the floor of the attic above us. Most unusual, the attic was 'finished off' back in the late 1700s, the walls made of costly bead board paneling with names of people carved in wood. Antiques bought for the children as they grew would cause nightmares. We bought a 1700s rope bed (and roped it) for our son, and he started spiking mysterious 104-degree fevers. We were constantly rushing him to the hospital. He started telling us about the people who would come and play with him when he was sleeping. After about a year of this, we got rid of the bed, and the fevers and 'visits' stopped. We had purchased the house from a couple who had been experiencing financial difficulty, and we ended up meeting some people who knew them and said that those prior owners were desperate to get out of the house because everything began going wrong for them when they started living in the house.

"Within six months of our moving into the house, we also began experiencing weird financial difficulties. These would continue until we moved out. We were at our wit's end about the house and our belief that it was causing us financial difficulties. After a sudden, fascinating, and almost unbelievable intercession by the Blessed Mother, and solely on the strength of that intercession (yes, it was that powerful), we converted to the Catholic faith. After our conversion, the house's attacks on us increased. Prayer would cause it to abate for a bit, and we didn't understand at the time the use of Holy Water and blessed salt. When we finally decided to sell it, the house was angry. We could feel it. We prayed for protection and deliverance. We prayed for the future owners. We told our broker about what went on the house. She wasn't surprised. She said every psychic will tell you that Newburyport is more haunted that Salem. How seriously did we take the curse of this 'beautiful' antique home and the costly antiques we filled it with? The weekend prior to the closing of the sale we put everything we owned—yes everything, except our clothing and family pictures—out on the sidewalk with a 'free' sign. Local antique dealers quickly found out and descended. They were dumbfounded by what we were doing. Everything was gone in one and a half hours. Towels, bed linens, pillows, and personal care items were thrown out. We were taking none of it into our 'new life.' I dropped off our clothes at a local laundromat to be cleaned. We stayed with my mother for the two weeks between the sale of our old home and purchase of our new home. Before I would let any of my family walk through the front door of the new house, I hired a cleaning crew to do a heavy duty cleaning. We purchased the 'spiritual warfare' kit and every corner, window sill, and closet was sprinkled with salt and Holy Water. That was before the priest arrived. Our financial problems and attacks ceased from the time we moved out of the old house and have not returned."

7

'I've Been to the Beyond and It Is Beautiful Over There'

Why there are such negatives is mysterious. Was it the former owners haunting it?

Most "ghosts" are more benevolent. A famous rock singer, Billy Joel, of Long Island, New York, recounted that "I used to live in East Hampton, and it was an old house that had been renovated, and I was going to bed one night, and I walked into my bedroom and I saw what looked like a woman brushing her hair in front of a mirror. She was very old-fashioned-looking—it looked like a 19th-century woman in a dressing gown. It was quite realistic. It was quite three-dimensional. I wasn't dreaming. I saw this. It lasted for about a minute."

Souls can get caught between realities. Such spirits don't mean to scare us. A Mass should be said. We are not to keep them around. We are never to initiate contact. Through prayer we are to free them.

There are the famous stories of ghostly hitchhikers, endless cemetery accounts, and whole towns (such as Savannah, Georgia) that feel "haunted."

There are haunted convents, and churches, and monasteries. In Italy, Padre Pio cited the example of a deceased young monk who had been neglectful of his monastery duties and as a result was haunting the chapel (where St. Pio saw his spirit knock over a candelabra as the "ghost" was cleaning the altar in reparation).

Hauntings occur because souls have not been set free or because there has been dark activity.

We die in the reality and state of mind in which we lived.

A dark mind heads for a dark place.

A tainted one heads for what is gray.

The goal: to avoid unpleasant steps on the way to splendor.

"The way to escape the void is to choose love and light over the darkness," concluded Kevin Williams, a near-death researcher.

For most, there is the glimpse of paradise.

There is no more fear of death.

It's the greatest joy in life.

At times, in near-death episodes, it seems like everyone goes to Heaven.

But death must come in God's timing and we do not get to Heaven as a final destination until our lives have been purified.

Still, the transition to another life is far easier (if we prepare) than the most optimistic expectation.

"It is impossible that anything so natural, so necessary, and so universal as death should ever have been designed by Providence as an evil to mankind," said famed author Jonathan Swift.

"I never felt better," were the parting words of Douglas Fairbanks.

By the mercy of God, the deceased, as already indicated, are usually there to assist us.

This is one of the most glorious aspects of "dying": the reunion with everyone we knew during life on earth. And not by way of a haunting!

It can happen before the tunnel, during transport, inside the tunnel, or at the end of the passage. It can also happen before death actually comes. There are so-called "deathbed visions," documented at great length by Dr. Karlis Osis and Dr. Erlendur Haraldsson in a study of 640 medical observers (doctors and nurses) who had witnessed a total of 35,540 patients on their deathbeds and reported that 1,318 of them saw apparitions, 884 encountered visions, and 753 experienced striking elevation of mood—*often brightening out of the depths* of depression or pain as they found themselves in the transcendent presence of people they had known and loved: the dearest of the dear, demonstrating to us again that at every turn God has a mercy we can't imagine.

Let's stay on this issue of deceased loved ones:

In the Osis and Haraldsson study, what was seen was not the result of drugs, fever, or brain damage—despite medical claims that such visions are the result of delusions as a person nears the end. "The frequency analyses clearly indicate that the majority of apparition cases cannot be readily explained by such medical factors as high temperature, hallucinogenic diseases, the administration of drugs that could produce hallucinations—for example, morphine, Demerol—or by hallucinogenic factors in the patient's history," wrote the researchers in 1977. "Of those 425 patients on whom we have information concerning medication, 61 percent had received no sedation at all. Furthermore, nineteen percent of our patients had received such small doses or such weak drugs that our respondents did not consider them to have been psychologically affected. Thus, eighty percent of the terminal patients who had had apparition experiences during their illnesses were not affected by drugs. This means that only one-fifth were considered to have been influenced by the medication. Of these, the largest group was the 'mildly affected' patients, a category where it is likely that the drug was not the main cause of the hallucination. Only one percent were strongly affected by the sedation, and eight percent moderately affected.

"A second physiological factor which could induce hallucinations is high fever, because elevated temperatures are sometimes known to bring on a delirious state. We received information on the temperatures of 442 of the total 471 patients. Of those, fifty-eight percent had normal temperatures and thirty-four percent had low-grade fevers of up to 103 degree. Only eight percent of the patients had high temperatures of 103 degrees or more." Nor were stroke, brain injury, or uremic diseases a major factor. In ninety percent of such occurrences, the deathbed apparitions or visions were of parents, spouses, siblings, children, or someone similarly close.

"In the course of our research, we quite often encountered reports of a sudden rise in the patient's mood shortly before death," reported the researchers, who wrote a book on their study called *At the Hour of Death*. "These inner changes in patients are at times so profound that they scare some medical observers and change the lives of others."

Some saw angels. Some Jesus. In certain cases, saints like the Blessed Mother or St. Joseph were reported. A Catholic woman in her thirties who was critically ill with pneumonia "had a picture of the Blessed Mother facing her," reported one medical observer to Osis and Haraldsson. "She was gazing at the picture. Later she told me that Mary had come out of the picture and said, 'Don't be afraid. I don't need you yet. I will come back later.' This woman had a new baby to care for. She was happy to see Mary—it was so beautiful to see. At first she associated the experience with death, but then she felt relieved—it wasn't her time."

A heart attack patient in her sixties with a devotion to St. Joseph saw that holy figure and said he wanted "her to come to him, but she was unwilling.

"She told him that she still had things to do, that she would stay in bed and get better. The apparition calmed her. She was serene and peaceful, in a religious sense, and she began to get better several hours later."

"The apparitions 'seen' by the dying are predominantly experienced as guides assisting them in their transition to another mode of existence," said Osis and Haraldsson. "A typical example would be the following case of an eleven-year-old girl with a congenital heart malady. 'She was having another bad episode with her heart, and said that she saw her mother in a pretty white dress and that her mother had one just like it for her. She was very happy and smiling, told me to let her get up and go over there—her mother was ready to take her on a trip.' The vision lasted for half an hour. It left the girl serene and peaceful until her death, four hours later. The unusual part of this case is that the girl never knew her mother, who had died when giving birth to her. She certainly did not have a chance to grow emotionally close to her mother, as most of us do. Yet, when that last hour came, her mother 'was there.'

"Encounters with ostensible messengers from the other world seemed to be so gratifying that the value of this life was easily outweighed."

The cases happen whether the dying person is old or middle-aged or a child.

When the parents of a youngster are still alive, it is often the grandparents—if they are deceased—who are witnessed. In one account in the survey, the appearance of an apparition to a businessman caused pain to turn into serenity. "It was an experience of meeting someone whom he deeply loved," said the report. "He smiled, reached up, and held out his hands. The expression on his face was one of joy. I asked him what he saw. He said his wife was standing right there and waiting for him. It looked as though there was a river and she was on the other side, waiting for him to come across. He became very quiet and peaceful—serenity of a religious kind. He was no longer afraid. He died a very peaceful death."

The figures emerge out of light, or are simply in the room.

Those who go beyond the deathbed to the other side, of course, also have the reunion. They may see their loved ones on a meadow, near a lake, or across a river (representing the "divide"). Or, a deceased loved one may be in a house the dying recognizes but *doesn't* recognize (that seems familiar, yet not something that's actually in a physical memory). The relatives are usually described as healthy, whole, and youthful—in their twenties or thirties—despite what may have been disfiguration or old age (when they were last seen on earth).

Remarkably, some medical personnel report that they themselves have witnessed apparitions.

Sitting at the side of a dying 15-year-old son, one mother reported that she sensed something behind her. "I kept turning around and looking," she said. "The sensation grew stronger each time I turned around. The third or fourth time I turned, I saw my father—who had passed away thirteen years ago, standing in the doorway of my son's room. He was big as life. I saw such detail. I even remember seeing his shoelaces. He appeared to be brown and gold in color and there was a glow around his body."

As for angels, they have been cited in the literature for centuries.

Like loved ones, they come to escort the dying beyond the threshold. They take a situation that is supposed to be so black and terrifying and turn it into elation.

In fact, the heavenly beings seen by dying patients are likely but the tip of the iceberg; the room may be full of unseen spiritual activity. Often, there is more than one angel. Our prayers *empower* them. They split the veil.

Meanwhile, when we pray for the deceased, the Blessed Mother once said, they can see us. And seeing us, they intercede.

"My mother died when I was only a year old," a fellow named James M. Donahue of Aston, Pennsylvania, wrote to me. "She was killed by a drunk driver. My father raised seven children by himself. He never remarried. I can remember coming home on leave and finding my father clutching my mother's picture crying. My father was always the strong silent type but you always knew he loved you.

"I had seen him go through hell since my mother passed. He never forgot her or stopped loving her. I should also mention mother was extremely devoted to Our Lady. She worked as a nurse at a children's hospital. On holidays she would bring meals to the homeless. Everyone told me she was a saint. He missed her terribly. He came back from a cruise and said his arm hurt. My sister, who is also a nurse, went with him to the hospital. They did an emergency bypass operation and all seemed to be fine. My dad was in the recovery room laughing and joking with my sister and the other nurses *when all of a sudden he said he didn't feel right*. My sister was asked to leave the room as they worked frantically to save him.

"But it was just his time! When my sister was informed of my father's passing, the nurse said, 'I know this probably doesn't mean anything, but your father was saying something before he died. We couldn't make it out so we asked him what he was saying. He looked up at us with a smile and said, 'Oh, I'm sorry. I was just talking to my wife.' Keep in mind this all happened so fast that the nurses knew nothing about our family history. I should also mention that the day my father was buried was my mother's birthday! Coincidence? You tell me. I have no doubt whatsoever that my mother's birthday gift was to be reunited with her husband in Heaven! Can you think of any better present than to have your husband back after twenty-eight years?"

8

Where the Light Is

There are joys we don't even imagine.

"I am a hospice volunteer for over thirteen years now and have been with many beautiful patients at the time of their passing," said a woman named Christine Rossi. "They have told me who they have seen and the faces are full of peace and joy. One lady saw the children that she had miscarried but they were not babies but little beautiful children running around her bed. My own dad reached both of his hands into the air and said, 'Welcome . . . it is so good to see you in person.' Most of these visions happen within 24 to 48 hours of our passing, and the way the angels are standing is meaningful too. If they are standing with their arms folded, it is a comfort visit to let them know that they are not alone and need to pack their bags for the journey. If the angel has his-her arms out (it is not a real arm, but two streams of light where our arms would be), then it is very close to passing."

In some cases the dying are "held" back by the prayers of those on earth—at times against their will.

"My grandmother was declared dead by the doctor who had tried to resuscitate her after surgery," another woman wrote. "A close friend, a nurse, was attending her. The nurse-friend screamed, 'Katie come back! Katie come back!' Grandmother did not want to return. She was in the vacuum tube to eternity and she felt free and happy, free of pain, free of worry. But she was called back: 'Katie, come back!' The friend grabbed her and began shaking her, 'Katie come back!' Grandmother heard the voice and, reluctantly she returned from the tunnel of light."

"Joan, I have been over there, over to the beyond, and it is beautiful over there," said another dying fellow. "I want to stay, but I can't as long as you keep praying for me to stay with you. Your prayers are holding me over here. Please don't pray anymore."

The lesson: prayer must always be oriented to what is best for those approaching death, and what is in the Will of God. *"Your Will be done."* Release and pray. Release when it is the person's time. You will see the person again.

When we don't pray in a way that best benefits those approaching the threshold we miss an opportunity to help in a valuable way.

That's the Light. There is also the darkness. This comes when we have not lived or loved as we should.

Thus, preparation for death must be our highest priority.

That path will bring joy—both during life, and at the end of it.

Humility. Faith. Love.

Without those, we step into darkness.

The art professor I mentioned, Howard Storm, who died in 1985, had been an atheist—and a militant one. He hated religion. He went so far as to make fun of a Baptist secretary. He told a nun who wanted to take one of his art classes that it was okay—she could take his course—but only if she didn't discuss God.

When he nearly died (from a ruptured duodenum during a tour of museums in Paris), Dr. Storm found himself in a foggy passage that sloped downward with half-human creatures who viciously harassed him (until, despite his "non-belief," he cried out to Jesus). He later learned that the nun had been praying for him daily. "As I lay on the ground, my tormentors swarming around me, a voice came from my chest," recalled Dr. Storm of the attack on him by hideous creatures. "It sounded like my voice, but it wasn't a deliberate thought from my mind. I didn't say it. The voice that sounded like my voice, but wasn't, said, 'Pray to God.'"

He did and was saved.

Others have not been so lucky and find themselves in the lower reaches of purgatory or hell itself. There are countless levels in the afterlife, just as there are countless conditions in souls—billions of them.

At those lower reaches of purgatory can be a firelike hell and even the harassment of demons—although now the soul is saved. This is the region for souls who have committed extremely serious offenses (especially offenses against love) and have not expiated—meaning that they have not encountered the time or suffering needed to purge. "If you could only know what I suffer!" said the deceased nun in Church-approved revelations in a French cloister during the nineteenth-century (to a living nun). "Pray for me, please. I suffer intensely everywhere. My God, how merciful You are! No one can imagine what purgatory is like. Be kind and take pity on the poor souls. Do not reject the Way of the Cross. While on earth you will frequently suffer in body and soul, and often in both together. It is so beautiful in Heaven. There is a great distance between purgatory and Heaven. We are privileged at times to catch a glimpse of the joys of the blessed in paradise, but it is almost a punishment. It makes us yearn to see God. In Heaven, it is pure delight; in purgatory, profound darkness."

One Jewish man who died and came back told of seeing his sins like a swarm of avenging angels.

In Italy is even a museum with accounts and artifacts related to purgatory, including burn marks of hands or fingerprints on books, linens, or clothes.

At the bottom is darkness (or fire) while the middle region or "great purgatory" is described more like a huge room full of mist or fogginess and the upper reaches as closely resembling Heaven (but for the lack of His constant Presence). There is no clock time, but it can go on for "decades."

Thus, every moment we spend on earth is invaluable. Once in eternity, we will wish we could have known what we now hear and see laid out before us. What we will see is that everything was a gift—that our victories and defeats were all meant to teach us lessons, especially our sufferings (which cause us to learn faster than we normally would). Each minute on earth should be cherished.

"Watch carefully over your interior life," said the purgatorial nun. "Keep all your small troubles for Jesus alone. He is well able to make up to you for whatever He takes from you. Your life must be one of unceasing interior acts of love and mortification, but God alone must know of it. Do nothing extraordinary. Lead a very hidden life, yet one closely united to Jesus. Jesus wants you to love Him alone. If you put no obstacle in the way, He has extraordinary graces to bestow upon you, such as He has never yet given to anyone. He loves you in a special manner. Be always very humble. Lead a hidden life. Do not busy yourself with anyone. Attend to your own sanctification and affairs."

There is one preparation that is invaluable and it is knowing that all reduces to love, humility, and unselfishness. As a woman from Midway City, California, named

Diana Cunningham recounted: "I was baptized as a baby Catholic and grew up sporadically attending Mass with my parents. But, I never went to Sunday school or had any formal education in the faith. And in my teenage years, I fell from the faith after discovering the 'truth' of evolution. I became an atheist. Then, in my first year in college, I became agnostic, after I did something radical—I prayed and it was answered! This opened the door a crack to belief in God again, which lead me to dabble in things I shouldn't have, such as the New Age.

"And so, this was the spiritual state I was in when I had my 'near-death' experience.

"It happened while I was undergoing surgery.

"I was twenty-two years old and living in Syracuse, New York, and I had broken my tibia and fibula. I was scheduled for surgery to place a rod in the major bone.

"And I was deeply scared. I had never had surgery before, and I knew that even in simple surgeries, things could go wrong and people could die. I was agnostic, but being very frightened as to what might possibly happen, I recalled that in situations like this, one calls a priest.

"So, I asked my mom to find me a Catholic priest and she got the hospital priest to visit me right before the surgery. But, being very ignorant of the Catholic faith, I didn't know anything about what he was going to do. I just wanted some words of wisdom—anything comforting. I had no idea what Confession was or that I needed to tell him anything. I had no clue what the Anointing of the Sick was either. But the priest was very understanding. He did give me words of wisdom, as I had expected; then he gave me the anointing anyways. And wonderfully—strangely—enough, the healing oils made me feel a lot better. I just felt somehow I was 'ok' with God.

"They wheeled me into surgery. I slipped into uncon-sciousness. *Now, I don't know how long* I was actually unconscious in surgery, but sometime during this passage of time, I suddenly found myself awake and skipping in a vast field of wild flowers. Awake is a good word to use, because I kept becoming more spiritually 'awake' as I began noticing things in such wonder and awe. As I skipped along, I looked down at myself. I noticed that I could move again—my leg was no longer broken and I was fascinated with my hands: that I had fingers in this spiritual body I seemed to find myself in.

"I was wearing a bright yellow dress with a carnation print in deep red. The colors were so vivid to me. I noticed the green grass being so brilliant—a color green I have never seen here on earth. It was like neon but was such an 'alive' color, it is so hard to describe.

"In fact, everything seemed to me to be so alive—including myself—as I never felt more alive in my life. Life here on earth is like being asleep in comparison to what I was feeling. I was so awake that it was like being reborn. And as I became more awake, I began to notice that there were others in this place, too. In fact, I sensed someone off to my side, escorting me, but I was not given the ability to see this person. Now, I know that this person was my guardian angel.

"However, I was permitted to see someone else. As I skipped, I sensed someone behind me, and so, I turned my back and noticed this person—which I instantly knew was a demon—chasing me. The demon had taken a grotesque appearance of my boyfriend at the time. He was surrounded by a dense black cloud, which I also instantly knew were all the sins that I had ever committed in my life. I also knew that the demon had appeared as my boyfriend because my major sins involved lust and sins of the flesh. And as I noticed him, the demon reached out to grab me, though I also knew that he could never catch me in my skipping— that I was safe from him. *I then looked ahead* and noticed that the vast field was surrounded by a very dense gray cloud. I was skipping towards it. As I noticed the gray mist, I suddenly realized that I really wanted to reach it. Somehow, I knew that if I reached this gray mist, I would be able to stay. For a brief moment, it became my goal, but then, I began to notice something that made me so dumbstruck that I didn't notice it from the very beginning. As I skipped towards the dense gray cloud, I began to realize the profound Presence of God in this place that I was in. I looked up into a brilliant Light that should have blinded me.

"*The Light permeated everything* and I realized that this Light was what gave life to and sustained all the things I saw in this place. I realized that this bright Light was coming from God. I realized that God was real and that He existed. In the same instant, I realized that God resided in a place called 'Heaven' and that this Light was emanating from His Presence there. I also realized—instantly—that I was not in Heaven and that I was not in hell. In fact, I didn't know where I was, but I knew at that very moment that I wanted to go to Heaven!

"And when I realized that I was not in Heaven and that God was in Heaven, I heard in the very depths of my soul, a single question. God asked me: 'Do you love me?'

"And when He asked me that question, I threw every-thing—my heart, my mind, my soul into my answer to Him. I said '*yes*' from the core of my being. I wanted to stay and be with God. I had no care to come back to earth or my family or friends at all, because I had never been so ecstati-cally happy in my entire life as during my experience in this 'otherworldly' place.

"I was unbelievably, incredibly happy. Nothing on earth can compare to how I felt. If all the happiness I had ever had in my life were contained, it would be a mere drop in a vast ocean as to how happy I felt while in this place. And I also knew that if I made it to Heaven, I would be even happier than I was ever even in this place that I experienced. I knew that my ultimate happiness was to be with God and I wanted to be with Him. *But, once I said 'yes,' I was pulled from the place I was in*, towards the sky, at a very quick pace. The Light surrounding the vast field began fading and coalescing with other softer white lights, as I was being pulled through a tunnel of light. And then, with a shock, I found myself back in my physical body. With my eyes still shut, I could see the sharp and glaring artificial surgical light shining upon me.

"The doctor was waking me up in the surgery room. And I was waking up to the most excruciating pain I had ever had in my life. Two weeks later, I tried to approach my surgeon with this 'otherworldly' experience. He was not receptive to hearing anything about it, and for the longest time, I kept silent about it, though constantly pondering it in my heart. In my discoveries I came across a description about a place that was written down by a great saint hundreds of years ago. I can't remember the name of the saint, but it exactly described the place that I had been—the vast field, the surrounding gray mist. It talked about this place being beneath the earth, which made sense with the direction of the tunnel of light that I had been pulled up through—that the place was not Heaven, but certainly not hell, since it still had the Presence of God. I realized that I had been in purgatory. And then, everything began to make sense to me. The Anointing of the Sick—which enabled me to even go there—the demon and all my sins in that black cloud that I saw—everything finally made sense."

Countless are the rungs in this middle ground.

There is brightness to match the brightness we have and darkness where there is still gray in the soul. Sin, says Scripture, to repeat (*1 Corinthians* 15), is the "sting of death."

The problem, said the Kansas woman I quoted earlier, "is that most of us just don't know how to love. We are full of pride, jealousy, lust, and an almost insatiable craving for money and power. Television is full of this garbage. Why this is I don't know, but we are going to have to pay for this self-centered and unloving behavior toward one another, whether in this life or the next one. I think we pay for it now, though, right here on earth, because if you don't know how to love, you can't experience the joy of living."

After death, that realization becomes visible.

There must be whiteness within to see whiteness around us.

We smudge our souls with blots of dark with every single negative (including criticism).

A key to eternity is in watching each thought (a single one of which can trip you up).

Through practice, through struggle at first, but eventually through habit, we can train ourselves to look at the best in life, to think well of others, and to love.

Having seen Heaven, and God's Light, those who die now know for certain that they will exist forever and that God loves them more than they knew anyone could love anyone else—vastly more—but they have to purify every fault in order to remain in His constant love, His constant Light, His constant Presence.

9

Secret Knowledge

It's a Presence no one wants to leave (save those in need of purification) and some are given a choice of whether to return.

Before a final destination—in other words—certain souls are allowed a decision.

"This place will always be here waiting for you, and if you want to stay now, I will accept you," the Lord told one near-deather.

"I want to return for my children," is the usual reason why anyone chooses *not* to enter eternity; usually, they want to stay.

"My wife needs me," might be another concern.

In the majority of cases, there is no decision.

"You have work to do."

"Your mission is not yet complete."

"Your life is unfinished."

"It is not your time."

"Not now, daughter," the Lord told a Catholic doctor in California who died in her early twenties.

"It's not time for you to be here now, but when it is I will be there," said a father to a daughter who nearly passed to the other side.

"Are you prepared to die?" might be a question posed by the Being of Light.

"What have you done with your life to show me?"

"What have you done with your life that is sufficient?"

One man went up a staircase into a room where men sat and discussed whether he should be sent back.

"You *must* go," RaNelle's grandmother told her.

A peculiar account comes from a gentleman in Bedford, New Hampshire, named Clement Nadeau who told me he "was at work checking some electrical components when I came in contact with 370 volts and I was immediately in another place.

"I was in a large, semi-dark room and was looking at a large wooden door, like one from a castle. As I was preparing to go through it, I looked to my right and saw a group of six older white-bearded men in white robes standing in a semi-circle. They were discussing something with another older man whom I somehow recognized. As I moved toward them, they gestured me to leave. When I looked at the waving hand of the lead person I was immediately thrown back into my body and felt the pain of the electrocution."

These are actual testimonies.

Those who return long to be back in that place where they felt peace like they did not know peace but realize that life is a gift which must be accepted totally, vigorously, and with daily enthusiasm.

They no longer *fear* dying—they look forward to it—but the last thing they would do is cut it short.

On the other side, secret knowledge was imparted to them, and though they are not allowed—upon return—to recall all the details, the subconscious knows new truths and recognizes the tremendous opportunity to advance through all the challenges of earth.

The worst thing, they now know, would be to toss the gift of life away.

They are almost uniformly against war and capital punishment and euthanasia and anything that infringes on God's life-giving deigns.

They would never commit suicide.

They are against abortion—the ones with legitimate encounters.

Why don't they remember more?

Many are frustrated with an "amnesia" that occurs when they return. They know something but *don't* know it—can't put their fingers on certain things.

That's because having too much knowledge of one's purpose on earth would compromise the test and thwart spiritual development. Also, we might rush things—and fumble. It is what was known to the Greeks as the "River of Forgetfulness."

Some are allowed to know aspects of their future.

"At that moment there was a 'TV screen,'" said another experiencer. "It showed me that I would have a prolonged period of physical pain for myself; it showed me that members of my family would suffer physical pain; it showed me that my sister-in-law would die prematurely, and she did. The Presence said, 'You will go back and hold your family together; you will be the cement.'"

"Go back. Your work on earth has not been completed. Go back now."

"It is not yet your time to come here."

How some struggle to remain! They argue that it's too beautiful where they now find themselves—too full of love

—to exit. They can't take the thought of earth, its blindness, its nastiness. They *fight* to stay. Or—as has often happened—they get mad at the doctors when suddenly they find themselves back in the physical. Some have actually shouted at surgeons. It is a burden. They have lost the freedom. They have lost the vision of splendor. Returning to the body feels like putting old soiled clothes back on.

"When my brother was two years old he was taken to the hospital with bronchial pneumonia and a 108-degree temperature," a woman named Kristin King of Plainfield, Illinois, wrote me. "The doctors were certain he would die. My mother and father had called a priest to come in to administer Last Rites. Shortly after, my brother was pronounced dead for about two or three minutes. He slowly recovered and was sent home. Of course my parents were elated. Since my brother was the youngest, and had actually died, my mother did not let him leave her side.

"One day while she was ironing and he was at her feet playing—I believe it was Bishop [Fulton] Sheen on the television—she and my brother paused to pray (as much as a two-and-a-half year old can). When the prayer was done, my brother said, 'I know Jesus. He was with me when I was sick.' My mother stopped everything and started to further question him. 'Jesus and I were in a field by a river,' he told her. 'I wanted to stay with him and play. Then we were watching you from the ceiling mama, and you were crying, and father was there. Jesus told me that you needed me, so I could not stay and play, but that I would be able to come back later, after I did what I was supposed to.'"

Once the decision is made to return, it occurs in a flash. Suddenly they are back in bed or in an operating room. Often it's the precise moment when doctors and nurses have frantically resuscitated them.

One young woman who nearly died said she was told by "messengers" that she had to stay to help her children because Satan has "such great power on earth."

You have been placed where you are for a reason and great souls are planted by God at all levels of society for mysterious purposes.

There is the sense that life must be lived to the fullest, to the fairest, rooting for everyone to succeed, since we are all tied to the same Plan.

"I was in the emergency room and there was a code red. I flat-lined," says Barry Charles Karl Moravek, a business executive from Richland, Washington, who "died" in 1997 from an allergic reaction to penicillin. "I floated above my body and I saw my wife and she was panicking. They said they lost me and I could hear it. I was right there—but on the other side. It's right there. It's right next to you, like the other side of a curtain. I found myself in front of a throne with the most beautiful Person I have ever seen for a short time.

"Then I was hurled—pulled up, grabbed by both shoulders and through a white light a long distance.

"Maybe there was an angel on each side of me. The light was purity. There is no earthly point of context in describing it. It was a beautiful light and what happened next was seeing what was like a light moving from behind or around a planet and radiating like birth and it was purity.

"It was so wonderful and beautiful and everything in my life was suddenly perfect: it was joy and bliss and a Person materialized.

"He was in clothes but not like any clothes I could explain. His body was radiating light like nothing I had ever seen before.

"Then I saw my grandfather in a perfect body and communicating in thought and there was this realization and heightened awareness of *everything*. I had answers to things that were the opposite of what I would have thought.

"Next there was the loudest Voice I have heard, and it called out my name—*Barry*. It reverberated to my soul. I was in the middle of the voice and the voice was in the middle of me!

"It dealt with my life. My mother believed that, when we die, we sleep until judgment. It's what I was taught. But there I was and all of a sudden I was connected to people to my left who were running through every moment of my life. None of this experience would I have subscribed to before. At super speed I saw my whole life with the judges off to the left. They were judges but they *weren't* judges. They weren't judgmental. They just showed me (my life) and I posed the question: why did I have to be born? It's something I used to ask as a kid when I was depressed.

"They showed me that the spirit always exists but there was this total dark and excruciating emptiness and it was lonely and more. It was traumatic, frightening, like I first was shown Heaven, then hell. I can't explain what it was about. In a twinkling it was explained to me that I was at the end of time and also at the beginning. I had full under-standing and was given a choice to stay or go back and I was running out of time and finally decided to come back and I fell a *gazillion* miles back into my body.

"When I got back, they were using [electric-shock] paddles on me. I jumped a foot off the table. I was flipping like a fish on a dock. I had been dead for twelve minutes and had started 'going' again. I was full of epinephrine and it caused a huge shock and my heart had been speeding. I had been given way beyond the regular dose as a last-ditch measure. When I died, it was like the weight of the world was off my shoulders. The joy. The release. The connection. The freedom. The major lesson I took from it was, 'Praise Jesus. Worship Jesus."

10

How Jesus Speaks

Let go.

Release to Him.

Only then is there peace.

How often do we do that (here on earth)?

Let disputes—insults—pass by. Ignore them. Forgive. Do not ignore evil, but don't judge. Be neutral. Cast out all evil effects (jealousies, spiritual attacks) and in the Name of Jesus send them to the foot of the Cross, for disposal according to God's Will. Seal yourself. Root out all pride. Take nothing personally. Care not about your ego. Only then are you healed and only when you are healed can you properly love.

And when you do, you find a new awareness—as those who see the other side report a stunning new ability to perceive.

It is not just a new perception of spiritual realities. It is even a new way of seeing what exists in the physical world. Fascinating it is to consider that St. Paul may have had a near-death experience (*2 Corinthians* 12 again) that informed his preachings!

Some near-deathers describe how, when they returned, they were suddenly aware of every blade of grass—could see light in each. Perception became acute. They could see a spiritual essence, a spiritual halo around things. Everything is interconnected, not occult-like, but in the personal Force of the Lord.

In tune with Him, we perceive much more even of the physical reality. We think we know what "awake" means, but when we die, we will be aware in a way we never imagined. There is a hyper-perception, contrary to the idea of "sleeping in death." Those who rise out of their bodies say they could look down and not only see their bodies and those working on them but could see their own bodies *from every angle* at the same time, in a completely different perspective.

After the tunnel, in the Light, on the other side, the communication is "telepathic." When Jesus speaks—say countless experiencers—His Voice is just right there in one's head.

In Heaven, thoughts are heard. There is no need for movement of lips. Questions are answered instantly. "It was astonishing, the speed with which I was learning," said the woman named Elane. "Knowledge that had somehow slumbered deep in my soul was released, and I was extremely exhilarated by the reawakened knowledge.

"Light and knowledge were flowing into me from every direction.

"I could feel it. Every part of my body was reverberating with the light gushing in. Even my fingertips were receptors of light and knowledge. It was as if I were drinking from a fully-engaged fire hydrant."

"His Light began to fill my mind, and my questions were answered even before I fully asked them," noted a woman from Seattle. "His Light *was* knowledge. It had power to fill me with all truth. As I gained confidence and let the light flow into me, my questions came faster than I thought possible, and they were just as quickly answered."

"I could hear, as I had never heard in my life before," a woman told another researcher. "I could hear the soft whisper of winds in the trees below me. I could hear the ripple and tinkle of many running waters. I could hear the distant shouts of children at play, and the joyous barking of a dog. I could hear the singing of many birds in the trees below. I had not heard the singing of birds for many years."

When people act out of their greed, they emit an energy that serves to destroy the harmony within nature, while saying "thank you"—being grateful—has the opposite effect.

An atmosphere of *gratitude* results in the highest brilliance.

Thus we see that the supernatural weaves in and around our reality but we are blind to it until we make the transition.

It's on the other side that we look back and see that this reality was lit by the power of God—and that what we saw in the physical was the underside of needlepoint.

It is the knots. It is the side that is unsightly.

"At that point I just started heading toward that Light with my being—I don't know how—and I was surrounded by what I would describe as a tunnel," the Long Island woman had recounted to me. "There were like rings of wind, like the funnel of a tornado, and it was moving forward.

"Besides the Light, which was very bright, there was a prism within it and music unlike any that there is on earth. I don't know how to explain it. The music was so welcoming, and it becomes a part of you. It was comforting, angelic. And I was moving up this tunnel and getting closer and closer to this Light. I know there was some kind of companion with me because every time that I had a thought to ask a question, everything was answered immediately, as I 'asked' it.

"I remember stopping briefly because within the walls of this tunnel were beings. I never had a great religious upbringing and never thought of purgatory, but when I came back it seemed like part of that, probably the last level of purgatory. [The souls] were existing like on the outside of the tunnel and resting as if they were sitting or standing or lying down.

"I had a surge of emotions. I felt sorrow for them and despair because they were stuck where they were but it was also made very clear to me that as much as there was despair, there was full knowledge and peace within [these souls] because they understood and accepted that they couldn't yet move forward."

"Brilliant, brilliant," said this witness, relating the Light she also encountered. "You can't describe it. It was just filled with love and peace and the knowledge of God. As you move through that tunnel, you're more and more consumed by it. And then at that point I was in the Presence of the Lord. I was prostrate. I was not able to withstand the awesomeness and the majesty of what was before me! I was nothingness compared to that. And then there was a period of being embraced by this love and peace and serenity and knowing I had reached my final destination—that *this* was truly a home."

Pope Benedict XVI described Heaven as "the dwelling place from which we came."

But we get "home" only after the "test of love." That's what earth is: a place where it can be so difficult to feel good about others, and yet a place where we must learn certain lessons, often the hard way. "Although our spirit bodies are full of light, truth, and love, they must constantly overcome the flesh, and this strengthens them," noted a famous experiencer named Betty Eadie whose death was both fascinating and controversial and previously quoted. "Those who are truly developed will find a perfect harmony between their flesh and spirits, a harmony that will bless them with peace and give them the ability to help others. I was told by the Savior that [Heaven] could be compared to one of our photographic prints. The spirit creation would be like a sharp, brilliant print, and the earth would be like its dark negative. This earth is only a shadow of the beauty and glory of its spirit creation, but it is what we needed for our growth."

Listen to a woman who died in a head-on collision on Columbus Day in 1985:

"I was driving down a road and the other car was coming the other way and at the last moment he decided to turn left right in front of me. I said, *'Oh my God he's tu---* 'I didn't even have time to say 'turning.' The next thing I knew I was looking down at the top of my car.

"I looked down and I saw my car crunched and the guy get out of his car, come over to mine, and shut the lights off. I didn't know until later what *that* was all about. But I suddenly lost interest in what was going on down there— *because I saw this white light* and there was this tunnel that seemed very dark, with this great light at the end. I really wanted to find out what was on the other side. There was this *feeling* coming through of *love*. I just sort of thought, *'I want to go through that,'* and the next thing—I was through it!

"And I was in this place but it wasn't a place. It was an environment, an atmosphere. It was love. And it was amazing. It was total bliss, total joy, total love. Total acceptance: total, 'everything is fine and always will be and always has been.' It felt like home; it felt like where I belonged! . . ."

"The next thing I knew, I was standing in the middle of a circle of these 12-foot beings of light. They were pretty intimidating—but not really. They felt more like family than the deceased relatives I saw.

"It seemed to go on for this timeless period," she testified on YouTube. "And I really wanted to stay, because it was *really* good there. It felt like the Heart of God. Next thing, I woke up in the emergency room at the hospital. 'What happened?' I asked. I felt like I was tossed [back] like a stone," she said. On the other side "you realize that the most important thing is love—the *only* thing is love. All that petty stuff doesn't matter. We all know we came back with a mission. Mine is to be here in three dimensions in this time and this space and hold the energy of the Light of God—just hold it. As we hold it, we help other people around us find it."

It is the Light of love. It is also the Light that vivifies us.

It surrounds us, engulfs us, and directs the body's amazing systems. Have you ever wondered at the way your body can know how to heal a wound, or respond to countless circumstances flung its way by the hostility of our planet?

Many are those who have lost a limb and yet still "feel" it. That is the spiritual body.

On the other side, they will look whole and young.

This is another constant theme: that relatives and friends encountered after death appear as they were in their prime, as I said, from twenty-five to thirty, perhaps forty— slim and in the state of total well-being. There are no longer wounds. There are no longer the ravages of age. There is no sickness—no sign of it, not in Heaven: no more of that constant struggle between light and dark, goodness and nastiness—the tussle that makes every day a challenge of patience (and often like walking through molasses).

Remarkably, after death, the blind can now see. There have been cases where the sightless have been able to intricately describe the medical instruments, their color, and even the clothes worn by medical personnel who were urgently resuscitating them, as I alluded. When they glimpse the other side they see relatives they never could see while they were living and one can only imagine the surprise. We can see in every direction. In that reality, *we see from all angles.* The senses have no limitation. Such will be the iridescent light that it will be hard to tell where the edge of a plant—glowing as it does—ends.

"It's hard to describe, but somehow the spirit body combined the youth and vigor of twenty-one-year-olds with a sense of perfect maturity," noted another who saw beyond our realm. "All their faces look fresh," added one more, "like the faces of very healthy people who are out of doors all the time."

There is what we might call a sparkle that makes up the attire, although terminology again falls short of what is witnessed. It is a level of comeliness for which we have no earthly parallel, and thus no adjectives. The most gorgeous portraits of Mary and Heaven are rejected by witnesses as poor attempts at conveying the beauty of Mary in apparition.

It can not be done because it is beyond the realm of our experience.

One seer described the Blessed Mother's attire as "shimmering" and "a different color than we are used to seeing on earth. For special feasts the Blessed Mother sometimes wears dresses that are of gold, and her veil is of gold, and she has many jewels. She appears in a radiant light and disappears as the light fades. I have never seen any painting or statue or picture that looks like the Blessed Mother. [She] has a beauty that is unlike anything on earth. When she smiles, I feel such joy! Her beauty and presence are beyond my ability to describe!"

It was a vision of paradise—of this ineffable realm—that caused Thomas Aquinas to say that you could toss out many of his theological ruminations now that he had actually seen what so many speculate about. It changed his life. "Such secrets have been revealed to me that all I have written now appears of little value," he said in 1273. The visions are powerful. But even at its most sublime, believed Pope Gregory, who studied near-death episodes, the experience of visions involved the role of an intermediate mental capacity, in which Divine illumination mixed with sensory impressions. In other words, he saw near-death experiences as real but involving symbolic images. Indeed, a case he studied involved a man who "saw" a ship waiting to take him away.

There may also be symbols in the modern episodes, although the consistency in certain details indicates the encounter is beyond simple metaphor.

There are the living waters and perhaps a pond with pure water against which our souls are matched. Are we similarly pure—ready for it?

Said a "born-again" woman named Choo Thomas from Tacoma, Washington, "Flowers of every type and description formed a sea of beauty everywhere I looked. I noticed that a variety of fruit trees grew close to the rock wall. These trees were filled with the biggest, most luscious-looking fruits I'd ever seen. They were ringed by a magnificent profusion of lovely flowers. Scattered throughout this amazing garden were huge, gray boulders that seemed to be strategically placed for sitting and resting. The pond really intrigued me, and as soon as I saw it, I began to sing in the Spirit and to dance for joy. I can't really explain why I reacted to the scene with such enthusiasm, but something supernatural was propelling me to express my gratitude, happiness, and peace in a demonstrable way. The Lord sat on a rock and watched me dance. I recalled a verse from the Old Testament: 'Then David danced before the Lord with all his might' (2 *Samuel* 6:14).

"He, the Lord, spoke to me, *'This is a special pond.'* I knew it was, but I could not understand why. The Lord did not explain His statement to me at that moment, but I surmised that the pond held many spiritual secrets that I would eventually learn, one by one. I wondered: Is this where my sins, and the sins of all other believers, have been buried? Is the pond a symbol of the water of the Word of God?'"

On the other side, they say, are those dozens of primary colors—each more resplendent than anything encountered on the most resplendent day in the most extravagant landscape, no longer combinations of red, yellow, and blue.

It is as Scripture says: "Things which eye has not seen and ear has not heard, and which have not entered the heart of man, all that God has prepared for those who love Him" (*1 Corinthians* 2:8-10).

Betty said it is like comparing a brilliant photographic print to a negative.

But there are times when the dead are in need and manifest so that we remember them. When Thomas Edison died, the clocks of two associates stopped at the exact time of his passing. His own grandfather's clock stopped a few minutes later.

"I was an oncology nurse and intensive care nurse for years and witnessed many patients' death experiences," Mary Powell wrote me. "There are several that I never forgot.

"One was a seventyish man. I had just come on the evening shift and was evaluating him as he was in and out of consciousness. While I was at his bedside, his eyes widened and he became terribly agitated. He said, 'Look, the devil is here!' Immediately I blessed him with water, made the Sign of the Cross on his forehead, and said the prayer to St. Joseph, to whom I have always had a devotion [and who is the patron of the dying]. He became less agitated and went back into his deep state of unconsciousness. The next evening when I came to work, the staff said he died about midnight and was very peaceful.

"Another patient was an alcoholic and dying the slow death that comes with years of alcohol abuse. I was giving him his evening bath and he was very agitated, with a look of terror. I blessed him and said the prayer to St. Joseph and St. Michael and he began to calm down."

"There was a young man of about thirty who had been brought to the house who was dying of AIDS," wrote another, Mary Woods. "He had lost his vision, and was unresponsive most of the time.

"When I realized that he was in the final stages of dying, I contacted his family and some of them came. I was talking to his sister and helping her to accept the process that she was experiencing, when her brother started kicking and flaying his arms and legs, and seemed to be fighting someone or something off.

"It was very frightening! He continued to do this for about twenty minutes, when at last his breathing became very shallow, and less and less when his spirit left his body.

"It was the most frightening thing I have ever seen. You could almost see the evil ones pulling on him!"

The "valley of the shadow of death"?

There is nothing, say the vast majority, to fear.

The shadow passes quickly; the valley is resplendent. *Virtually all emphasis is on the Light.*

"Amazing." "Beautiful."

"It was a funny feeling," a woman named Linda told a medical doctor. "I was in a lot of pain before I blacked out. Then all of a sudden I was looking down at my body! But at the same time, it wasn't like I was really out of my body looking down. I was in it and out of it at the same time.

"I couldn't see anything that was being done to my body. I couldn't see the rest of the room or anything. All I could see was myself lying on the floor. Also I had a very peaceful feeling, like nothing had really happened to me at all."

11

Seeing Everything That Ever Happened to You

Once out of the body, our thoughts, like our senses, can go in infinite directions at the same time.

It is a "judgment" and yet not a judgment: in the review of life, transgressions are revealed more as lessons.

There is not a single thing that ever happened or was said or that even was *thought* that is not in our record.

Our sins may have been confessed, and thus forgiven. "A part of me began to anticipate certain events, things in my life I would dread seeing again," said RaNelle. "But most didn't show up, and I understood that I had taken responsibility for these actions and had repented of them."

The review is often conducted by Jesus, angels, or men who appear more ancient than ancient. They do so with total understanding.

You will need to tell them nothing.

Nothing can be hidden upon death, and yet the Lord will not be there to embarrass you. He simply shows us in the truth of His Light.

This can occur at any time during the transition. It can occur in the tunnel, at the *end* of the tunnel, or after a little tour of the other side. It can take place immediately upon release from the body, or during the last moments of life.

"My every thought and deed of my lifetime was portrayed in a rapid three-dimensional panorama," recalled another who was clinically dead. "I felt as if everybody around me knew my every thought."

"It was like I got to see some good things I had done and some mistakes I had made, and you try to understand them," said a third. "It was like: 'Okay, here's why you had the accident. Here's why this happened.' It all had meaning."

"All of my faults were revealed so very graphically in front of me," is another testimony.

Here are others:

"The best thing I can compare it to is a series of pictures, like very high-quality color slides. It was just like someone was clicking the slides on and off in front of me, very quickly. It was all so fast."

"I could see all the mean things I did as a child. I was a real mean little kid! I wished that I hadn't done these things and wished I could go back and undo them."

"My whole life flashed across my mind. I saw myself crying as I went to school in the first grade. It was very, very real, and I was there!"

"I was watching my whole life being replayed just like on a color TV set."

"I was not only shown the things I did good and bad, but like a three-way view," said the woman from Long Island. "I was seeing it first through my eyes and how offensive it was. I was seeing it through the eyes of the person I had offended. Then I saw through the eyes of Jesus. When you see it through somebody else's eyes, you see how it intertwined with their lives. You see it from a whole different point of view and how it affected their journey. And then when you see it through the eyes of the Lord, you see it as a whole. It makes the whole thing complete. You see how in the course of all creation it made a difference and how it then affected the Creator—how it stops at the Creator when you offended one of His own."

The whole world is not worth a single harsh word.

What counts to God is going to startle you.

"The Lord showed me the things that really mattered, the 'extraordinarily,' 'magnificent' things that I had done," said this same woman, who asked me to call her only Barbara. "There were two profound examples. One was when my girlfriend lost her fiancé and it was devastating. He had been decapitated in a car accident, and the Lord showed me how I was on the phone with her one day for two or two-and-a-half hours and just sat there and listened to everything that she said.

"I remember saying to the Lord, 'I don't understand. I didn't say anything. What great magnificent deed did I do?' I could never comprehend how this was something extraordinary or magnificent. I did nothing. I just sat there. I didn't say much more than five or six words. I couldn't comprehend how that could be so pleasing to the Heart and Mind of Our Lord.

"Then I was shown another time that I had walked into church and this woman had lost her husband. I didn't know this woman, but I was so moved that she had lost her spouse that sitting in the pew I felt I had to do or say something and so after Mass I had just gone up to the altar—she had been sitting in the front—and just put my hand on her shoulder. Again, I didn't say anything to her. It wasn't what I said. The Lord made it very clear that it was the gesture, the placing of my left hand on her shoulder." This He considered a magnificent achievement.

"It was like there was a judgment being made and then, all of a sudden, the light became dimmer, and there was a conversation, not in words, but in thoughts," said another who will never forget it. "It showed me not only what I had done but even how what I had done had affected other people. It wasn't like I was looking at a movie projector because I could feel these things; there was feeling, and particularly since I was with this knowledge . . . I found out that not even your thoughts are lost . . . Every thought was there. Your thoughts are not lost."

"When I was in the company of Jesus and the angels, they asked me if I would like to see my life," recounted Dr. Storm. "Unsure of what to expect, I agreed. The record of my life was their record, not my memory of my life. We watched and experienced episodes that were from the point of view of a third party. The scenes they showed me were often incidents I had forgotten. They showed me effects on people's lives of which I had no previous knowledge. They reported thoughts and feelings of people I had interacted with which I had been unaware of at the time. They showed me scenes from my life that I would not have chosen, and they eliminated scenes from my life that I wanted them to see. It was a complete surprise how my life history was presented before us. Seven angels and myself held by Jesus were arranged in a circle while the scenes were projected in the midst of the circle. It was similar to a play without scenery except for the bare essentials."

It is not great feats the Lord is looking for—not great feats as men describe great feats.

The Lord cared about how Howard had made others feel —dwelt on that—and skimmed right past "achievements" such as winning a shot-put championship.

"Nobody has the same journey," continued the Long Island witness, Barbara. "My whole experience had so much to do with where I was in my personal life. It had a lot to do with my children and my husband. The way I was offending the Lord the most at this point in my life was my nearly verbal abuse. It was my attitude and the way I spoke to my husband and children. It was my tone and the things that I said that were very offending to another's soul and heart. You can be firm with your kids, but the Lord doesn't want you to use an insulting tone. We don't see things the way the Lord does, and for me it was a tremendous eye-opener. I was shown my vocabulary and the tone with which I said things, because it was a condescending tone. Firmness is allowed—but with love."

Barbara was also shown how particular events had a tremendous rippling effect—far more than she imagined. When she woke up grumpy and was negative to her husband and kids, the Lord showed her how this spread to them and from them to others through the day: at the workplace, at the deli, at stores, and then through the families of those who were touched by the negativity until many had been affected.

"There was a circle of light around the world," she told me, "and as I awoke and did this, the circle of darkness went over this circle of light and erased it. Then I was shown the opposite, how when I got up in the morning and smiled and presented breakfast, hugging the children, how it went from my house—a drop of light that started in this one spot on the globe and went in this band of light around the globe, which is the way it is supposed to be."

In some cases, it's like a drama, with just a few items to define the time and place in one's life. With others, each scene comes alive.

Some see every single thing that ever happened to them while others like Storm see certain select chronological events.

In reviewing athletic "achievements," God is not interested in who won and by how much but in how teammates encouraged, helped, or hurt one another.

A huge mistake: choosing career success over success as a human being.

Dr. Ritchie recalled seeing what looked like an enormous mural with figures that were three-dimensional (moving and speaking). He was surrounded by it.

Many of the figures were *him.*

"Transfixed, I stared at myself standing at the blackboard in a third-grade spelling class, receiving my Eagle badge in front of my scout troop, wheeling Papa Dabney onto the verandah at Moss Side," he wrote. "I saw myself as a two-and-a-half pound infant, panting for breath in an incubator. Simultaneously (there seemed to be no earlier, no later), I saw myself lifted by Caesarian section from the womb of the ill and dying young woman whom I had never laid eyes on before."

"There were other scenes, hundreds, thousands, all illuminated by that searing Light, in an existence where time seemed to have ceased. Every detail of twenty years of living was there to be looked at," he testified—in an experience that sparked modern research into near-death episodes. "The good, the bad, the high points, the run-of-the-mill. And with this all-inclusive view came a question. It was implicit in every scene and, like the scenes themselves, seemed to proceed from the living Light beside me. *What did you do with your life?*"

What had he done with the precious time he was allotted?

Ritchie was shown how for him religion had turned into smugness and self-esteem (that he was better than kids who didn't go to church) and how his motive for going to medical school was to afford a Cadillac.

Searching for an example in what he now realized had been "an endless, shortsighted, clamorous concern" for himself, Dr. Ritchie recalled the "accomplishment" of becoming an Eagle Scout.

"That glorified you," the Light replied.

The fornication, adultery, addictions, and gluttony will all factor in (the Lord needs us to purge those before we can remain in His Presence), but more than anything He evaluates us on how much we have loved and served others—in whatever way (large or small) He has set before us.

Knowing this, we can be prepared now—we can rectify the past—so that our life reviews are not like an exam to which we arrive unprepared (having studied for the wrong test).

In the afterlife, in reviewing your life, you will even hear the thoughts people had in situations that pertained to you and the reasons they said or acted as they did. In the Light, you will forgive everyone. To attach to a hurt would place a distance between your spirit and His—which, once you encounter it, you now will never want to stray from again.

We accept where we belong without dispute and do not want to enter His Kingdom until the robe we are given has been whitened to perfection.

"I didn't actually see anyone judging me," said another. "It was more like judging myself on what I did and how that affected everyone."

You will relive every time you showed any empathy.

Remember that every day for the rest of your life and you will have a good chance at entry.

Approach every decision with the thought of how it will look in your review. "Incidents appeared in my life where I had succeeded in a competitive environment and gotten ahead of someone else," testified Elane Durham. "I had not intentionally hurt other people, but my competitive success had the same effect as though I had. Their sense of rejection was evident to me, and I could feel their hurt also. While I was enveloped by the Light, I knew the answers to the questions that had formulated in my mind. Secrets from the beginning of time to infinity were clear to me. Myriads of things were understandable. I understood, for example, that when I left earth I would leave with whatever spiritual growth I had attained there, and I would take that spiritual growth with me into this new world."

12

Into a Distant Light

In the Light of the afterworld, earth looks vastly different and we see that many basic premises we held were wrong. Success in God's Eyes is not success in the eyes of the world. In the afterlife we will see that it was not right to gouge, to compete without mercy, to seek a larger, better house, a bigger pool, for the sake of feeling superior.

We will see how wrong it is to look down on others because of religion, social standing, or "importance."

Only God knows why someone is whatever religion that someone is and if in error on certain points, many religions have aspects that help the progress of those who adhere to them, and so we are not to judge. They may teach discipline better than other religions, or sexual purity, or be more instructive on spiritual warfare. The Catholic reach is the highest and has as its highest calling love.

"Having received this knowledge, I knew that we have no right to criticize any church or religion in any way," said the Seattle woman I have quoted. "Very special people with important missions have been placed in all countries, in all religions, in every station of life, that they might touch others."

Does this mean we do not correct? It doesn't mean anything of the sort. We are called to correct, for example, aethiests. We are called to evangelize our faith. We are called to demonstrate the incredible transcendental power of Christianity, which can lead to the higher realms of Heaven—that realm of the saints—when practiced properly.

Do we purify our hearts during Communion? Do we sincerely repent through Confession? Do we pray to be selfless? Do we ask the Blessed Mother to guide us toward the best spot in the afterworld—do we do this on a constant basis?

During the Rosary, do we ask for help in completing the mysterious mission that God has assigned us?

It is important to have strictures but not for the sake of strictures and not to the point where we bind ourselves to a legalism that binds us to the earth.

Let us recall how Jesus rebuked the Pharisees because they followed the letter of the law but not its spirit.

The gifts of the Church must be expanded through *discipline*. Discipline, it turns out, is a key to eternity, and we discipline ourselves when we resolve not to talk again against our neighbors, seek selfish gain, or have lustful thoughts. Peace is your road marker.

Nothing should be done to an extreme because it knocks us off balance.

This too is a very important key. Are we *balanced*? Are we living the full Catholic faith (or just the rituals)? Are we tending to all aspects of life?

If there is any extreme it should be only an extreme love for Jesus.

Here we find balance. Here we also find mercy.

Time after time, those who return from the brink of death say they lost their fear because they found God to be far more merciful and understanding than they expected.

The main trait of Jesus is a love so powerful that it rises above any experience of love and nearly necessitates a new word.

It is a love that will bowl us over (in the most pleasant sense of that term) and be felt in every part of our beings.

There will always be a sense of that mercy. One near-deather recalled: "As the events of my life proceeded, and I felt the distress of others, this Being of Love communicated the thought: *'That's because of the society you were raised in. You behaved in this way, in part, because of the way you were raised. And that is not enough to keep you from the Presence of God. You did not turn your back on God.'*"

Only the Lord knows the obstacles we face and thus judgment is His alone.

It will be inherent in His Light. It will be automatic. It will be just *there*, before us.

Your soul will be illuminated instantly.

A theologian named Father Reginald Garrigou-Lagrange once noted that "at the moment of separation, the soul knows itself without medium. It is enlightened, decisively and inevitably, on all its merits and demerits. It sees its state without possibility of error, sees all that it has thought, desired, said, and done, both in good and in evil. It sees all the good it has omitted. Memory and conscience penetrate its entire moral and spiritual life, even to the minutest details."

The Light will be similar to the light that converted Saul and in it will be the Truth as we have never seen it— somehow comforting, despite our flaws. You will feel a release with it.

"When I would see something, when I would experience a past event, it was like I was seeing it through eyes with omnipotent knowledge, guiding me, and helping me to see," one man told Dr. Moody. "That's the part that has stuck with me, because it showed me not only what I had done but even how what I had done had affected other people. And it wasn't like I was looking at a movie projector because I could feel these things; there was feeling, and particularly since I was with this knowledge, I found out that not even your thoughts are lost. Every thought was there. Your thoughts are not lost."

"This Being of Light surrounded me and showed me life," said another to a researcher named Dr. Melvin Morse, who wrote a book called *Transformed by the Light.* "Everything you do is there for you to evaluate. As unpleasant as some parts of it are for you to see, it feels so good to get it all out. I remember one particular incident in this review when, as a child, I yanked my little sister's Easter basket away from her because there was a toy in it that I wanted. Yet in the review, I felt feelings of disappointment and loss and rejection. I was the very people I hurt and I was the very people that I helped feel good."

As an Arizona woman looked down on her body, she could watch a priest giving her last rites. She could see everything.

"Behind me in the bed was a clock," she recalled. "It was up on the wall. I could see both myself in the bed and the clock, which read 11:11 a.m."

13

The Heart of God

After the tunnel—or *instead* of a tunnel—some find themselves journeying through clusters of stars, on the way to the
distant light—as if through space.

"It was like completely leaving the whole space-time
continuum," said an agnostic woman who died in a motorcycle accident in 1970 (thrown head first onto a Los Angeles
freeway). "There was this feeling of no distances and no
time and I was *so* alive, more alive *then* than I am now."

"We descended together from God's light into a universe
of bright stars," said the New York nightclub owner, of what
occurred after the tunnel experience. "We were again in the
deepest void of space, but now I felt comfortable in this
environment as well as in my spirit body, and I felt at home
in this celestial location. As [another soul] and I continued
to descend, I was startled by the magnificent ethereal structure directly below us. The heavenly structure resembled an
amphitheater similar to those found in ancient civilizations.
This amphitheater was made of a brilliant, crystal-like
substance that radiated multi-colored waves of energy
throughout its form. The amphitheater was suspended in
the void of space in the same fashion that a space station

might hover in space. The amphitheater was similar in size to a sports stadium and conveyed a great majesty."

It was then that he went through the review of his life.

This was strikingly similar to a Mormon who when she died entered "a room like an amphitheatre; it was slanted down. At the front of the room there was something that looked to be a table or an altar. As I looked at the front of the room I saw three men dressed in white. I knew where I was supposed to sit, and I came down the center aisle and sat on the left side, in toward the middle of the seats."

"When the double doors to the room would close, I knew that I would not remember what was behind those two doors—a veil would be placed over my mind," she recalled to Arvin Gibson in *Echoes from Eternity*. "But I wanted to remember this room, and I studied it carefully."

Through the walls, she saw earth suspended in space.

Note how an atom with its electrons and protons is like a solar system and perhaps it is that we go from one "atomic" realm—dimension, as I said—to another.

"Secrets from the beginning of time to infinity were clear to me," said another, as we discern. "Myriads of things were understandable. I understood, for example, that when I left earth I would leave with whatever spiritual growth I had attained there, and I would take that spiritual growth with me into this new world."

"While I was in the Savior's Presence, I was told and shown many things besides my life review," adds still one more from the many books on this subject. "Enormous amounts of information flowed into my mind—information that I have since forgotten. When I first arrived in the room, for example, He asked me if I had any questions. I did, and the moment the question was formulated, the answer was in my mind. Pure knowledge seemed to pour into me from Him."

On the other side, many are shown what God planned for them to accomplish and yet when they return there is only a sketchy memory.

There will be an unknown language, they tell us, but one we will understand. It is a language that was spoken when we were in the Heart of God. The knowledge will come like sun rays or music, which will flow across and throughout the surroundings. The music is immediately noticed. It is a defining characteristic. There will be no beat to it because in Heaven there is no time (and because the beat of earthly music is often the drum of darkness). In Heaven the music is different from any we have heard, save perhaps for the recesses of a dream. They call it the "music of the spheres." Perhaps Bach, or Beethoven, gave us snippets—tiny ones.

The music will flow as a force of ministry.

It is balm.

It will heal the spirit.

Truth is translated into song.

"There was a sound in the air that completely defies description," said one. "It was as if there were a multitude of voices, and a multitude of instruments, blended and playing soft music. The twittering of birds and other beautiful sounds were all melodically instrumented into the music that wafted through the air.

"All of the earth's symphonies pale in comparison," is an actual testimony. "It sounds loud and piercing as a trumpet, yet the notes glide smoothly as a violin and also a sweetly pitched as a flute. It is all these rich sounds blended perfectly as one. As I concentrated on the music, it gracefully slowed down to a soothing lullaby. The effect was the most beautiful and emotionally soothing song I have ever heard!"

Pure, soft music is the air of the other side.

Music is absorbed. It is digested. It vivifies. On earth, it affects us more than we realize.

It is the resonance of the soul and in Heaven it is only a good, a positive, an uplifting resonance.

Think wind chimes.

"Exquisite harmonies."

"A celestial choir."

"Sublimely beautiful."

"Unearthly tones."

Those who return say it was like the gardens, the leaves, the colors were singing.

"A thousand tiny golden bells."

"It flowed unobtrusively, like a glassy river, quietly worshipful, excitingly edifying, and totally comforting," said a near-deather, Richard Eby.

"High sweet tones."

"I found myself saying, 'Bach is only the beginning!'" said Dr. Ritchie.

In a chorus, the whisper: "Jesus."

This marks the entrance, as do visual effects. Gates and archways are described. So are meadows. There are walls. There are symbols of partition. It may be a river. It may be a row of hedges. I have mentioned this.

Once beyond, there is no return.

"Looming just over the heads of my reception committee stood an awesome gate interrupting a wall that faded out of sight in both directions," wrote Don Piper in *90 Minutes in Heaven*. "It struck me that the actual entrance was small in comparison to the massive gate itself. I stared, but I couldn't see the end of the walls in either direction. As I gazed upward, I couldn't see the top either. One thing did surprise me: On earth, whenever I thought of Heaven, I anticipated that one day I'd see a gate made of pearls, because the Bible refers to the gates of pearl. The gate wasn't made of pearls, but was pearlescent—perhaps *iridescent* may be more descriptive. To me, it looked as if someone had spread pearl icing on a cake. The gate glowed and shimmered. I paused and stared at the glorious hues and shimmering shades. The luminescence dazzled me, and I would have been content to stay at that spot. Yet I stepped forward as if being escorted into God's Presence."

In case after case, this is told to those who die: they will not be able to go back into their bodies if they reach a certain threshold, and so the decisions are made here. It is like a meeting place. It is perhaps a reception area. "The Being urged me to enter the light, and we went to another place, a different world bathed in light," testified a Utah resident. "Located in a large field was an enormous and beautiful gate. It had jewels on it and it was of a shining golden color. My guide pointed at it and said: 'That is the gate of Heaven.'"

There was a tall window made of purple stone, marble-like, said another, with light shining through—crystalline, though not really transparent.

"I wasn't blinded," said Piper, "but I was amazed that the luster and intensity continually increased. Strange as it seems, as brilliant as everything was, each time I stepped forward, the splendor increased. The farther I walked, the brighter the light. The light engulfed me, and I had the sense that I was being ushered into the Presence of God. Although our earthly eyes must gradually adjust to light or darkness, my heavenly eyes saw with absolute ease. In Heaven, each of our senses is immeasurably heightened to take it all in, and what a sensory celebration!"

"I ran across the grass, and my feet didn't touch the ground," another testifies. "I could feel the air around me—not that there was a lot of wind—just a refreshing feeling of the air. Power and energy were coming off everything. A man leaning against a tree motioned with his arm and said, 'Hurry, Elane. Everyone's waiting.'"

"Melodious."

"Harmonious."

The flow of music. The flow of beauty. The flow of knowledge.

There is total communication.

It is mental.

It is in the spirit.

Everyone is transparent.

There are no secrets in this realm.

Everything about us is known by everyone else—but with total understanding. Condescension is missing. Pretense is non-existent. Secrets of earth are shown. Those from whom secrets were kept hold no grudge. Empathy transcends everything. If one has remarried after the death of a spouse, the spouse totally understands. It is not an issue. She or he is still there for you. Those against whom you have sinned have long before forgiven everything—totally purging it before they entered this realm. Everything you have ever said or done is known to everyone without judgment.

On the other side, we are given robes, and their purity will reflect our purity.

In front of the Blessed Sacrament, we see the white of such cleanliness, and it is there—not with paganism, or the New Age, or other esoteric beliefs into which near-death people often find themselves diverted—that we see not only the cleanliness of what we will wear, but also find our missions.

"Woe to you, scribes and Pharisees, you hypocrites," says *Matthew* 23. "You cleanse the outside of cup and dish, but inside they are full of plunder and self-indulgence. Blind Pharisee, cleanse first the inside of the cup, so that the outside also may be clean."

Any jealousies, unforgiveness, or other sins will display themselves as blots on the robe, and no one will laugh, but you will want to clean your robe before residing permanently in Heaven among those who—like their surroundings—are immaculate.

"As we approached the people, I saw that they were weaving on large, ancient-looking looms," said Eadie. "My first impression was 'how archaic' to have manual looms in the spirit world. Standing by the looms were many spiritual beings, male and female, and they greeted me with smiles. They were delighted to see me and moved back from one of the looms to let me have a better look. They were anxious for me to see the workmanship of their hands. I went closer and picked up a piece of the cloth that they were weaving. Its appearance was like a mixture of spun glass and spun sugar. As I moved the cloth back and forth, it shimmered and sparkled, almost as though it were alive. The effect was startling. The material was opaque on one side, but when I turned it over I was able to see through it. Being transparent from one side and opaque on the other—similar to a two-way mirror—obviously had a purpose, but I wasn't told what the purpose was. The workers explained that the material would be made into clothing for those coming into the spirit world from earth."

Another recalled walking into the "living waters" and then coming out with a robe around her.

"I was dressed in a long white flowing gown," said Elane, who died in 1976. "The whiteness in the gown was different from any white I had seen before; there were depth and iridescence associated with it. It was an alive white, as were the other colors."

The robes are mainly white. Those on active chores of some type are seen as wearing immaculate pastels. There are pinks. There are yellows. During apparitions of the Virgin Mary, a shimmering gown is likewise described: a pastel or luminous "gray-like" but not really gray—not any color—and sometimes more like gold or turquoise.

Other times, she is a pure white brilliant form surrounded by an "immense light."

Always, there is luminosity. The very essence of the person is light. An energy construct recreates us—steps out of the physical shell, as if plugged into an outlet, at this place where, of course, there is no electricity. Everything is a prism from which spirit and colors explode. There are what seem like shards of brilliant dancing light. There are no shadows. "The scene was sacred beyond words, beyond expression, and those who have witnessed it keep it hidden in their hearts," said RaNelle. "My hand was clear, like transparent gel, but there was light coursing through it like clear blood. The light didn't run in irregular patterns as it would in veins; rather, the light shot through my hands like rays or beams. My whole hand sparkled with light."

Hair sparkles. Beards sparkle. Eyes beam. There is a brightness in a way that we can not know on earth. The Light takes us, heals us, loves us. For God is the Light and the Light is from Him and through everything. And every-thing loves the person who enters it—the sky, the plants: nothing is infirm here. There can be no decay. Everything is in full blossom. Everything is connected. Light, truth, and life, learned RaNelle, are created and sustained in love, which God gives it. We too give it love, and creation expands—it glows, it grows. Love is the power that gives action to all around it.

The less fear they had, these folks learned, the farther they went into the Light—that incredible, inconceivable luminosity which serves as the most common feature of all such experiences.

"I don't know how I got there, but I found myself in a beautiful country lane," notes another witness. "I was strolling down the lane slowly and I felt I had all the time in the world."

Choirs. Singing children. The "sound" of flowers blooming and grass growing!

"Presently they came to a park in which there were all kinds of beautiful trees bearing inviting fruit," says another of the many who have offered public witness. "Also flowers that delighted the eye and filled the air with fragrance."

14

Your Afterlife Will Reflect the Light or Dark in You

Revealed in this setting is the right way of love, transforming those who experience it.

"Being a former Pentecostal and earth dweller, I was always judging," said Linnie Smith. "God in His infinite mercy took my soulish heart and remolded the urge to judge. Oh, not that I don't fall into judging. Of course I do. But an I-love-you-the-way-you-are attitude just floods me in meeting people. It's like a balm of sweet, thick heavenly honey poured over it. A Kincaid painting reminds me of what I saw in Heaven. Just make it all alive and full of light-giving life, and you got it. Make music, the heavenly blend of birds, voices, instruments and bells and you're there. I stand beside myself and watch as this love unlocks the doors to hurting hearts, that this flood of Heaven's honey may pour in."

If we want to see Heaven, we catch glimpses in the splendor of nature around us.

If we want to see hell, we can see that too.

Hell is the opposite of love.

Is there a netherworld?

It's not a pleasant topic but to ignore it is to leave souls in danger.

From our saints to those who have glimpsed eternity we can say the following about the lowest realms: There is first off the darkness. It does not end with the tunnel. It begins there. Let's flash back to this for a moment.

As we have seen, in some descriptions, hell is like a dungeon, a musty, foul underworld where souls are trapped in "cells" and behind those bars harassed by demons. St. Teresa of Avila saw this at prayer one day "when suddenly, without knowing how, I found myself, as I thought, plunged right into hell. I realized that it was the Lord's Will that I should see the place which the devils had prepared for me there and which I had merited for my sins. This happened in the briefest space of time, but even if I were to live for many years, I believe it would be impossible for me to forget it. The entrance, I thought, resembled a very long, narrow passage, like a furnace, very low, dark, and closely confined; the ground seemed to be full of water which looked like filthy, evil-smelling mud, and in it were many wicked-looking reptiles. At the end there was a hollow place scooped out of a wall, like a cupboard, and it was here that I found myself in close confinement. But the sight of all this was pleasant by comparison with what I felt there. My feelings, I think, could not possibly be exaggerated, nor can anyone understand them. I felt fire within my soul the nature of which I am utterly incapable of describing. My bodily sufferings were so intolerable that, though in my life I have endured the severest sufferings of this kind—the worst it is possible to endure, the doctors say, such as the shrinking of the nerves during my paralysis and many and diverse more . . . in that pestilential spot, where I was quite powerless to hope for comfort, it was impossible to sit or lie, for there was no room to do so. I had been put in this place which looked like a hole in the wall, and those very walls, so terrible to the sight, bore down upon me and completely stifled me."

Hell is exactly what we have emphasized: a place of torment. It is the outward manifestation of hatred. Burning hatred. Sometimes there is fire. Worse than anything is the total absence of the Holy Spirit. It is what we form for ourselves when we live a hateful, selfish life. Most of all, it is for those who reject God.

Incredible it is that even at the very last moment, in that transition to the afterlife, at the tunnel—when the soul finally realizes that it survives death—are those so arrogant and spiteful as to still refuse Him, and thus hell is their choice. Those who are not comfortable with God gravitate to the muddiness of surroundings that match the dirtiness of their spirits. Such souls are not so much condemned as drawn here.

Some say only a tiny percent of those in near-death episodes have hellish experiences. Others argue that the figure is higher but that upon return the mind blocks it out. Surgeons have described patients who expired on the operating table and screamed in terror at what they had encountered when they were revived.

There is no nourishment; there is no warmth.

It is an outer darkness.

There are creatures.

Many kinds of demons haunt the condemned with features like those of gargoyles (or malformed humans). Their only delight is heaping hatred upon others and St. Teresa said that the affliction was worst than fictionalized accounts of "how the devils tear the flesh with their pincers."

We need not dwell on this for long. Fear is not productive, and those who love God have no reason to dread the lowest of reaches, or what Howard Storm described as "the cesspool of the universe."

Others depict the fire. During the famous visions at Fatima, Lucia dos Santos, the oldest seer, saw it as "demons and souls in human form, like transparent embers, all blackened or burnished bronze, floating about in the conflagration, now raised into the air by the flames that issued from within themselves together with great clouds of smoke, now falling back on every side like sparks in a huge fire, without weight or equilibrium, and amid shrieks and groans of pain and despair. The demons could be distinguished by their terrifying and repellent likeness to frightful and unknown animals, all black and transparent." Does this not hearken to the testimony cited previously?

"We could see people before they went into the fire, and then we could see them coming out of the fire," said a seer at Medjugorje. "Before they went into the fire they looked like normal people. The more they are against God's Will, the deeper they enter into the fire, and the deeper they go, the more they rage against Him. When they come out of the fire, they don't have human shape anymore; they are more like grotesque animals, but unlike any on earth."

Another visionary there saw a beautiful girl enter the flames; when she came out she was "no longer human."

"These creatures were once human beings," adds Dr. Storm, who was on his way down a foggy passage before he was saved by Jesus. "The best way I can describe them is to think of the worst imaginable person stripped of every impulse of compassion. Some of them seemed to tell others what to do, but I had no sense of there being any organization to the mayhem. They didn't appear to be controlled or directed by anyone. Simply, they were a mob of beings totally driven by unbridled cruelty. They had very long, sharp fingernails, and their teeth were longer than normal. I'd never been bitten by a human being before this. The level of noise was excruciating. Countless people laughed, yelled, and jeered. In the middle of the bedlam, I was the object of their desire. My torment was their excitement. The more I fought, the greater their thrill. They were playing with me just as a cat plays with a mouse. Every new assault brought howls of cacophonous laughter. I haven't described everything that happened. There are things I don't care to remember. In fact, much that occurred was simply too gruesome and disturbing to recall. I've spent years trying to suppress a lot of it. After the experience, whenever I did remember those details, I would become traumatized."

One female atheist who died during labor found herself "surrounded by a noise so loud and painful that it was like a giant freight train circling my head.

"At a deep level, I knew that this was going to be my 'eternal' condition. I was acutely aware of being alert and in a place of such darkness that my hand placed in front of my open eyes was impossible to see.

"There was no light of any kind anywhere. There was nothing in this dark, loud, chaotic place, but my thoughts and me. I was alone and in agony but I had what I would call expanded knowledge. It was like all the mysteries of the universe made sense to me and what we call important here in this life is mostly insignificant in the grand scheme of things. I sensed no one in this place but me and I knew that I would be spending eternity here alone and without peace." The question that kept entering her mind: *"What have you ever done in your life that was totally selfless?"*

"As I thought about the question I realized that I had always acted to please myself," she recalled. "I had never said a kind word or done a kind deed that wasn't motivated by personal gain."

In one survey twelve percent of near-deathers had hellish-like encounters, some with both mud *and* fire. One of these was a man named Don Brubaker who had a heart attack and found himself falling feet first into a damp, musty tunnel where he saw a huge glowing red ball "almost like the light on the front of a train.

"In that instant, as the red ball rushed toward me, I knew terror like never before," he wrote. "As it approached, I realized that it was really a large, eerie red eye. It stopped when it got close to me, and then began traveling alongside me through the tunnel. I could hardly stand to look at it, its gaze was so piercing."

That's hell and then—nearly overlapping—are the lower reaches of purgatory. This too is such a place of darkness—so like hell—that some near-death witnesses confuse it with condemnation.

There is a major difference: however horrible lowest purgatory may be, the soul there is saved and will one day ascend to Heaven.

But gloomy it is. The darkness there swirls around the feet and forms a barrier, holding those there prisoner, a darkness that in the words of Angie Fenimore was so thick it could be touched and "had life, some kind of intelligence that was purely negative, even evil."

"Everyone I saw was wearing dirty white robes," recalled Angie in her book. "Some people's were heavily soiled, while others' just appeared dingy with a few stains. Sitting next to me was a man who appeared to be about sixty years old. His hair was gray, and somehow I knew that his eyes were blue, even though everything here appeared in black and various shades of gray.

"This man's eyes were totally without comprehension. Pathetically squatting on the ground, draped in filthy white robes, he wasn't radiating anything, not even self-pity. I knew his soul had been rotting here forever. I was sure that this man had killed himself. His clothing suggested that he might have walked the earth during Jesus Christ's earthly ministry. I wondered if he was Judas Iscariot, who had betrayed the Savior and then hung himself. I felt embarrassed that I was thinking these things in his presence, where he could 'hear' me."

The word "purgatory," said Angie, was "whispered" to her (despite the fact, as I said, that she was Protestant). It was edge of the abyss and those who were there—contemplating their lives—radiated darkness as an aura. "Like oil over water, the active layer of spirits of light rested above a layer of grim, motionless dark beings," wrote Angie. "Drifting onto the plane, the newly deceased were dressed in white robes, but their gowns were dingy. Like silent sleepwalkers, these spellbound souls descended into the darkness, arms to their sides, their expressionless eyes locked in empty gazes. They came from the same direction that I had, dull and hopeless casualties of life that had banked on true death, continuing to fill in the back edge of the prison as the darkness expanded to accommodate them. So sad, they were so young and so dead. As I watched them filing down by the dozens, I was told that most of us who are dying now are going to a place of darkness. Hell, while also a specific dimension, is primarily a state of mind. When we die, we are bound by what we think. In mortality the more solid our thoughts become, as we act upon them—allowing darkness to develop in others and in ourselves—the more damning they are. I had been to hell long before I died, and I hadn't realized it because I had escaped many of the consequences up until the point that I took my life. When we die, our state of mind grows far more obvious because we are gathered together with those who think as we do."

Somehow areas of purgatory seem to branch from the tunnel where those who've received a glimpse have encountered what they describe as "bewildered souls."

There are the "dungeon" reaches and what has been described as the middle or "great" area of grayness, where most bound for purgatory head and where the greatest suffering—as in any part of purgatory—is God's absence. It is gray and ashen—the ashes of sins.

"I can tell you about the different degrees of purgatory because I have passed through them," said that deceased nun during the nineteenth-century revelations called *An Unpublished Manuscript on Purgatory.* "In the great purgatory there are several stages. In the lowest and most painful, like a temporary hell, are the sinners who have committed terrible crimes during life and whose death surprised them in that state. It was almost a miracle that they were saved, and often by the prayers of holy parents or other pious persons. Sometimes they did not even have time to confess their sins and the world thought them lost, but God, Whose mercy is infinite, gave them at the moment of death the contrition necessary for their salvation on account of one or more good actions which they performed during life. For such souls, purgatory is terrible. It is a real hell with this difference, that in hell they curse God, whereas we bless Him and thank Him for having saved us.

"Next to these come the souls, who though they did not commit great crimes like the others, were indifferent to God. They did not fulfill their Easter duties and were also converted at the point of death. Perhaps they were unable to receive Holy Communion. They are in purgatory for the long years of indifference. They suffer unheard of pains and are abandoned either without prayers or if they are said for them, they are not allowed to profit from them. There are in this stage of purgatory religious of both sexes, who were tepid, neglectful of their duties, indifferent toward Jesus, also priests who did not exercise their sacred ministry with the reverence due to the Sovereign Majesty and who did not instill the love of God sufficiently into the souls confided to their care.

"In the second purgatory are the souls of those who died with venial sins not fully expiated before death, or with mortal sins that have been forgiven but for which they have not made entire satisfaction to the Divine Justice. In this part of purgatory, there are also different degrees according to the merits of each soul. Thus the purgatory of the consecrated or of those who have received more abundant graces is longer and far more painful than that of ordinary people of the world.

"Lastly, there is the purgatory of desire which is called the *Threshold*. Very few escape this. To avoid it altogether, one must ardently desire Heaven and the Vision of God. That is rare, rarer than people think, because even pious people are afraid of God and have not, therefore, a sufficiently strong desire of going to Heaven. This purgatory has its very painful martyrdom like the others. The deprivation of our loving Jesus adds to the intense suffering. The majority of people go to purgatory. The lowest is close to hell and the highest gradually draws near to Heaven."

The threshold is a beauty to behold. Holy people may do their purgatory here—and it can be brief. In some cases, mere minutes. "You should see it here," said one voice from the beyond.

From here they look as from a cloud to the landscape of Heaven in the distance.

It is the waiting room.

It is the final laundering. It is far from the "outer darkness."

"In 1973, there was no mention of 'near-death' experiences," a woman named Marianne wrote me. "I never had heard of such a thing. But here is what happened in my dream: I was in a room, although there were no walls—I just knew it was a room. I was observing people in the room from the ceiling. Someone was with me—next to me. I did not see this 'someone,' just felt their presence. The people who I was observing were very happy. In my frame of reference, I thought they were having a party, although there was no food or drinks. The reason for thinking it was a party is that everyone was so happy. They were smiling and talking with a feeling of great expectation. Then just as suddenly, I was back in my body asking my obviously distraught mother what had happened to me.

"In later years, after hearing about near-death experiences, I took a second look at my own experience with a new point of reference. Now I had an understanding of what had occurred. It is my belief that I was shown the upper level of purgatory—where people are awaiting their entrance into Heaven. They were so happy, even joyous. Their appearance was young, healthy, and nicely dressed. I did not recognize anyone, but I only knew one person who had died and that was my great-grandfather. From what I knew about him, he may have needed more purgatory time—although that is not for anyone to say, only God.

"The person next to me showing me this place, my guide, must have been an angel.

"Since that time I have had a few 'angel' experiences and truly believe it was an angel showing me where, if I had died that day, I would have gone."

15

Why It Will Feel Like 'Home'

There are many mansions. There are hovels and huts and basements and small homes. There are lonely apartments. There are grand edifices. We move into our state of mind.

Everyone reading this has a chance to turn that state of mind into Heaven.

The very last decision a non-believer can make in a state of free will is whether he finally accepts the Lord now that he faces eternity.

There is that one last chance—which is why prayers must be said for the dying no matter how hostile they were to religion.

The Blessed Mother has said to *"pray daily for the souls in purgatory. For every soul, prayer and grace are necessary to reach God and the love of God. By doing this, dear children, you obtain new intercessors who will help you in life to realize that all the earthly things are not important for you, only Heaven is that for which it is necessary to strive. Therefore, dear children, pray without ceasing that you may be able to help yourselves and the others to whom your prayers will bring joy."* Sometimes the call for prayer comes in dreams, when the veil is thin.

"I want to share a very powerful story with you that occurred a little over a year ago," a woman from Shakopee, Minnesota, named Angela Howick, wrote me. "It begins with a dream I had.

"This dream was very different and I woke up with an intense desire to pray. I dreamed that I walked into a large room and it was filled with many deceased family members and friends. Although I could not see faces or physical bodies, I knew every single one of them. It was as if I knew their souls.

"I left the room and went down a small hallway. There in the hallway was my recently deceased uncle sitting on a bench. He was staring towards the sky and did not even look at me. I was very excited to see him and immediately said 'Freddy! What are you doing?' He responded in a very calm yet discontent voice, saying, 'I am waiting.' This was not the response I was expecting. My uncle was a very happy go-lucky, loud man who was always excited to see anyone. I asked him again, 'Freddy, what are you doing?'

"He looked down at me and we locked eyes. His response was the same: 'I am waiting.' He then continued to stare towards the sky.

"At that moment I knew what he was waiting for. He was waiting to be released from purgatory. In that moment I woke up and knew he needed prayers.

"A couple of weeks later, I called my aunt to discuss having a Gregorian Mass said for him. I was surprised to find out that she was actually having many Gregorian Masses said for several deceased relatives and friends. She had already called in the Masses, including one for my uncle. My aunt gave me the list of names and dates for when their Masses would start, so that I could unite my prayers and intentions with them. I wrote down all the names and dates.

"Later that night, I was praying and I realized that all of the names she had mentioned to me were the souls I saw in my dream. One particular name stood out for me. This was her father-in-law (let's call him Bert), a man who died before I was born. Even though I had never seen a picture of him or thought about him before, I know that he was in that room in my dream, along with all of the other people on the list for Masses.

"A few weeks later, I was praying the Chaplet of Divine Mercy, while driving to Mass, and when I got to the very last 'Holy God, Holy Mighty One, Holy Immortal One, have mercy on us and on the whole world,' I was overcome by an enormous sense of peace and joy. All of a sudden I started to cry because of this joy. I was not just shedding a few tears. I was wailing. I called out to the Lord, 'Why do I feel this way?' Then I heard three names: 'Freddy, Hermie, and Bert were released from purgatory.' I looked at the clock, 10:30 a.m. I knew that someone's Gregorian Masses were ending that day, but I couldn't remember whose. When I returned home, I looked at the list of names and dates and discovered that was the day the Masses for those three people had finished."

"I actually crossed over to another dimension where I was engulfed in a total feeling of love," claimed another woman. "I also experienced with extreme clarity why I had cancer, why I had come into this life in the first place, what role everyone in my family played in my life, in the grand scheme of things, and generally how life works. The clarity and understanding I obtained in this state was almost inde-scribable. I realized what a gift life is and that I was surrounded by loving spiritual beings who were always around me even when I did not know it. I was shown how illnesses start on an energetic level before they become physical. If I chose to go into life, the cancer would be gone from my energy, and my physical body would catch up very quickly. I then understood that when people have medical treatments for illnesses, it rids the illness only from their bodies but not from their energy, so the illness returns. I was shown that everything going on in our lives was dependent on this energy around us."

As we discern, we can know, surely, if nothing else, that spiritual forces define the physical and that we do not want to leave this world in bondage—for on the other side the bondage may be more pronounced.

Selfishness leads to the strongest shackles, or can abort a mission.

"You haven't given enough," said a voice to Mary Jo Rapini. "You can't stay."

We go to Heaven in accordance with those thoughts and deeds that contained no selfish motivations.

"In fact, our souls actually dwell not only within us, while we live on earth, but also in the spiritual realm we will find ourselves in after death," said a researcher I have quoted.

For some, time in the void is a simple time-out—a place before moving on to the threshold—while for others it is a taste of hell that seems never to end.

Those who pray avoid this—if they pray from the heart, if they pray unselfishly, if they love God.

Just thinking of God is enough to bring light and take a soul upward.

There is no hiding. There never was. It is not to be feared. Time and again, those who have died say that the angels didn't judge. They didn't scoff. They had perfect, unconditional love. They do not think less of us. They only want us to learn and purge so that we can ascend with them to the upper levels.

And here we come to a very key task in reaching the higher places on the other side: motivation. What is most acceptable to God are acts that involve no self-interest whatsoever. Actions done solely out of love for God are sacred deeds that bring eternal blessings.

"Perform all your labor as a selfless devotion to God, and that is how to make all your work holy," says a wise man.

Look at every thing as a devotion. If it is not offered up, there is not maximum credit. "This wisdom fully agrees with Catholic teaching," added the man just quoted. "Catholicism teaches that the only way to go straight to Heaven and skip purgatory is to die a martyr or become a living martyr. A living martyr is a truly crucified man—a totally selfless person; a living saint or apostle no longer serves their lower nature and becomes all good as Jesus and His Father are.

"The Eternal One showed me that, throughout my entire life, my ego had occupied the center stage of my life. I had lived solely for gratifying myself. I was motivated by varying degrees of self-interest in everything I did—although I had never consciously thought about this before.

"The whole world revolved around me. All of my actions were based upon some type of reward for myself—either tangible or intangible. So all of my actions were polluted by varying degrees of selfishness."

We find ourselves bound to whatever we inordinately possess. The degree varies with the extent of attachment. It can be with a thread, a rope, or chains.

Is this why "ghosts" are depicted with shackles?

At the scenes of murders or suicides spirits may linger in a confused state.

These spirits not only stall their redemption but can afflict the living.

Some may attach themselves to family members for generations.

Prayers for intercession of the Virgin can cleanse a house. We have Masses said. We ask Jesus to send them His Light.

Souls need to be released into the welcoming Light of the Father but many seem afraid. Others will not let go of the earth.

Focusing totally on God (and His Light) ensures quickest heavenly entry.

A sure path to the lower realm is arrogance.

God resists the proud and this means they are pushed back from Him in proportion to that haughtiness (anathema because it is a focus on self).

The vanity mirror has a skull in it.

The goal in life should be to purify before the end of this glorious test and to do so takes discipline (and discipline means moderation). When we're moderate in food, in drink, in play, in work, in spending, and in sexual activity, we have less to purge (and less that tempts us). Look at the rules of religions and you will find them aimed precisely at moderation.

There is the gray area. There is the outer edge. Some may be lost for minutes. Some for ages. If we pray, if we love Jesus, we can pass with joy. "Tell everybody that the key is to love," said RaNelle's grandmother on the other side. If one stays faithful to the Lord, acts like His warrior, disciplines the mind, "thereby not becoming distracted by the fleeting pleasures of life or caught in the cares of this life, which bleeds one's light," in the words of an experiencer named

Daniel, if one serves as tireless as possible in labor and devotions, with zeal, then one has an excellent opportunity to that entrance not only to Heaven but the higher realms.

Think simply. Don't speak more than you need to. Use that time to pray. Talk simply—and never in the form of gossip. Do not judge. *Judgment inhibits your ability to love.* Be holy and God will come to you and upon death you will be drawn to Him.

Never be discouraged. God does not expect you to be perfect right now; just improve a little each day and you are on the way to perfection.

Let God judge other religions. A great danger: spiritual pride. Let the beauty within define you. On the other side, you have the opportunity to be vastly more gorgeous than any person you have ever seen in the flesh. The Holy Spirit can show you how you would appear before God and how to work toward the best appearance. In Heaven, said one researcher I have quoted, we remember our real identity. Some say we have an eternal name. Some say it is different from here. Some see things as similar.

Knowledge will grow each day.

The answers to every mystery of earth will come as a flash and will pale beyond the new wonders that stretch across realms we didn't even know existed.

Only the best in us will survive, and as we approach God, we will find a joyful place, one where there is even hilarity (God has a splendid sense of humor).

"I felt the presence of millions like the stars at night before me, no existence of time, peace that cannot be experienced in our present state on earth, and the most beautiful, peaceful, love-filled voice that radiated all that is perfect engulfed my entire soul," said a correspondent who had a near-death dream.

From above, we will realize that there has been a war proceeding for a very long time on earth and that we have a special opportunity for God's favor because we live at a time when that battle is especially ferocious, increasing the merits of our struggles (which so often seem severe).

In Heaven, we are far away from that war and yet will observe matters on earth like a scroll that lifts the partition.

This is from actual testimony. We will intercede for those below in an atmosphere of bliss.

There are no misunderstandings in Heaven.

The coincidences of earth are the tapestry of Heaven.

Sweet Ripples. Sparkle shine wishes, is the way that Linnie put it.

"I am a very visual person, being an artist, yet there was nothing visual, just the sense of leaving my body and rising," I was informed by another. "As I was rising I felt the most peaceful, joyful, loving, fatherly Presence, which to this day is impossible for me to describe or explain."

16

In the Company of Your Angel

Everyone in Heaven will know who you are, and you will know every other person—if not from life on earth, in the instant recognition of heavenly knowledge. This is why it will feel like home.

"It is false to teach people that you are reborn many times and that you pass through different bodies," the Blessed Mother has said. "One is born only once. The body, drawn from the earth, decomposes after death. It never comes back to life again."

You will now look upon your earthly abode as a place of exile—just as the Church has taught, and just as it says in devotions.

Home.

"Suddenly I saw another path where all the dead members of my family appeared," said an experiencer named Diego Valencia. "It is the most wonderful, most peaceful place, there's no way to describe it," said a woman. "You don't talk with your lips. Whatever you think, God communicates with you. You know you're talking to God. The Lord said 'I want you to go back. I have something for you to do.' I said, 'Oh no, I don't want to leave this place!'"

In case after case, whether Catholic or Protestant (and often whether Christian or not), the Person of Jesus is seen as the very most impressive aspect of the experience.

It is precisely as the Bible has taught: that He is the intermediary between Heaven and earth, between God and humans.

It is His domain.

There are many complexities in Heaven but it is steadfast that a great Personage of Love greets the deceased and often is the One to give them a tour or answer their questions or place them in the company of angels.

The most striking feature in death accounts is virtually always that He is surrounded or consists of or exudes the most incredible light.

Dr. Ritchie had described the "welder's torch" and others strain to reach a similar comparison.

There *is* no comparison. The Lord—as we will see Him —is the essence of light itself.

"It was paradoxically absolutely everything," said yet another experiencer. "It included the entire universe that I was ever aware of. It was absolutely, positively everything. It was also absolutely the most beautiful thing that I've ever seen, that I've ever been near or experienced."

And so we call to Jesus.

Any other such light is a deception. All force comes from the Throne, where He is stationed at the Right Hand.

There is no force in science that is beyond the Holy Spirit—which is the "umbrella" power behind not only those forces we know on this earth—fire, electromagnetism, gravity—but ones we have not yet discovered (or that exist only in higher dimensions).

It is into those dimensions that we go as they unfold one into another.

"I saw galaxies and traveled to them with ease and almost instantaneous speed, visiting their worlds and meeting more children of our God," asserted the woman from Seattle.

There are levels. There are spheres. "Then we who are alive, who are left, shall be caught up together with them in the clouds to meet the Lord in the air; and so we shall always be with the Lord," states *1 Thessalonians* 4:17-18.

"There are also heavenly bodies and earthly bodies, but the glory of the heavenly is one, and the glory of the earthly is another," *1 Corinthians* (15:40) tells us. "I know a man in Christ who fourteen years ago—whether in the body I do not know, or out of the body I do not know, God knows—such a man was caught up to the third heaven," says *2 Corinthians* (12:2). There are spheres and we go to the sphere for which our spirits qualify. We go where we belong. We would have it no other way. At the highest spheres the light would be too intense unless we were prepared for it. That preparation is saintliness. "Those in the lower spheres could not have been happy in this higher kingdom until they qualified them-selves by a change of heart and mind," another notes.

Says *2 Corinthians* (5:1): "For we know that if the earthly tent which is our house is torn down, we have a building from God, a house not made with hands, eternal in the heavens."

Some say the "homes" in Heaven vary, as I noted, from little hovels to grand mansions, depending on the progress of a soul and the initial "judgment." There is a "council": some of those who have returned report that their life reviews were conducted by a group of elderly men or "ancients." "I was led to a room, which was exquisitely built and appointed," says the famous Seattle account. "I entered and saw a group of men seated around the long side of a kidney-shaped table. I was led to stand in front of them within the indented portion of the table. One thing struck me almost immediately; there were twelve men here—but no women. The men radiated love for me, and I felt instantly at peace with them. They leaned together to consult with each other. Then one of them spoke to me. He said that I had died prematurely and must return to earth. I felt them saying it was *important* that I return to earth, that I had a mission to fulfill, but I resisted it in my heart. This was my home, and I felt that nothing they could say would ever convince me to leave it. The men conferred again and asked me if I wanted to review my life. The request felt almost like a command. I hesitated; no one wants their mortal past to be reviewed in this place of purity and love. They told me that it was important for me to see it, so I agreed. A light appeared to one side, and I felt the Savior's love beside me."

Another who first saw Christ said she "went inside a set of double doors glowing with life. The inside was decorated with a wood paneling of 'living wood' from the trees growing at this wonderful place. He led me to some big double doors and told me to wait on this bench while he went inside. A bit later he came out of the room. He told me to go into the room and said he would wait for me and to not worry. He cautioned me to ensure I was truthful with the beings in the room. He said they were not judges, rather the ones who evaluated a soul's development based on a soul's history. He told me to remember who I was and to refrain from fear. I went in and saw a group of several spirits seated at a table. The table was made of the glowing wood and was perfect in every way. The spirits around this table had the highest vibration I had seen so far with the exception of Jesus."

There will be the constant surprise of seeing with new eyes and in a way that says: "but of course, I should have thought of that, I see now, it only makes sense."

"In the midst of my pain, I felt the love of the council come over me," said Eadie. "They watched my life with understanding and mercy. Everything about me was taken into consideration, how I was raised, the things I had been taught, the pain given me by others, the opportunities I had received or not received."

None of the events of our lives—none of what would seem far too embarrassing to share with anyone—seem to faze the beings of Heaven. They have seen it all. They know the temptations of earth. They have seen us naked—physically and spiritually. There is no denunciation; there is no shame. The reports are consistent. There is no harsh reprimand—not at this place.

We will see how angels orchestrated many events. We will see how opportunities opened up as we progressed. We will see the key to blessings. We will see what place and people were appointed for us—and how we strayed when we sought the *wrong* place or person.

Every person you encounter will be explained to you.

We will see your choices, and your desires, and the course of your life if all of your desires had been met.

"Oh, my goodness, I should have known!" you will say when you see what your earthly mission had been. "Of course. Oh, that's why such and such occurred. Oh, I see why that was arranged. Oh, my, I understand why those who were involved were involved—I see why I met everyone!"

We will see how angels intervened—some as actual strangers.

We will see that lust is the devil's version of love—because it is selfish.

What is rooted in pride will bring us the most distress.

Each day—while still on earth—we have the opportunity to beseech God and show us our lives as we will see them later.

135

We have the opportunity to do something extremely potent, and that is to treat every moment of life as it is our last.

We have the chance to look upon everything we say and do from the perspective of a life review—as if we are on a "stage."

Here is an important prayer from St. Teresa: O my God! Source of all mercy! I acknowledge Your sovereign power. While recalling the wasted years that are past, I believe that You, Lord, can in an instant turn this loss to gain. Miserable as I am, yet I firmly believe that You can do all things. Please restore to me the time lost, giving me Your grace, both now and in the future, that I may appear before You in 'wedding garments. Amen. (Prayer to Redeem Lost Time)."

This will orient our every action. It will pave a way that is golden.

Spend the rest of your life making others feel good and you will not fear the review of how you will live but will rather look forward to it!

The Holy Spirit can reveal you to you. In the important words of *1 Corinthians* 2: "The Spirit scrutinizes everything, even the depths of God. Among men, who knows what pertains to the man except his spirit that is within? Similarly, no one knows what pertains to God except the Spirit of God. We have not received the spirit of the world but the Spirit Who is from God, so that we may understand the things freely given us by God. And we speak about them not with words taught by human wisdom, but with words taught by the Spirit, describing spiritual realities in spiritual terms."

It is the hidden part of you that you must know and that through the sacraments you must cleanse.

Use the sacraments to build a heart of love.

That will get you there.

Music will surround you.

"They were making the most beautiful music I have ever heard," said Dr. Ritchie of the angels. "Bach, Brahms, Beethoven, Toscanini, all of the great musicians must have been able, in deep meditation, to have listened into this area and brought some of the music back into our own realm."

"As aware as I became of the joyous sounds and melodies that filled the air, I wasn't distracted," said Don Piper. "I felt as if the heavenly concert permeated every part of my being, and at the same time I focused on everything else around me. I never saw anything that produced the sound. I had the sense that whatever made the heavenly music was just above me, but I didn't look up. Myriads of sounds so filled my mind and heart that it's difficult to explain them. The most amazing one was the angels' wings. I didn't see them, but the sound was a beautiful, holy melody with a cadence that seemed never to stop. The swishing resounded as if it was a form of never-ending praise. A second sound remains, even today, the single most vivid memory I have of my entire heavenly experience. I call it music, but it differed from anything I had ever heard or even expect to hear on the earth. The melodies of praise filled the atmosphere. The nonstop intensity and endless variety overwhelmed me. The praise was unending, but the remarkable thing to me was that hundreds of songs were being sung at the same time—all of them worshipping God."

No song will hover upon sadness. There is no such emotion evoked in this realm. There will be ancient chants that at the same time seem brand new and beyond the capability of modern equipment (for the "instruments" here are unlike our instruments).

There is a precious aroma. Exotic, refreshing—similar but superior to what mystics know as the "odor of sanctity" (which is but a wisp of it).

The best of a rose or lily only begins to express the way this aroma will touch our spiritual senses—and once more, there will be the sensation of *ministry*.

All in Heaven edifies. All in Heaven gives health. Trees are august and towering and yet bear total symmetry—none growing beyond its place in a mosaic that could only be orchestrated by God.

It is a place of reception and also a place that ministers to those who are resting (taking a break from the tasks of God). Those who traverse do so with no rush because they have all the time of eternity, which of course means that there is no time at all—just the present. Past and future have found their way into one inconceivable package.

"In the distance, by the river there were six or seven people standing by some trees, and I could tell that they were waiting for me," said Elane, if we recall. "It was as if they knew I was coming. One of them looked up and said, 'There she is!' A man leaning against a tree motioned with his arm.

"All of them were dressed in white, a white which radiated light. Their hands and faces were not the same as on earth, but I recognized them quickly. They were about thirty years of age in appearance, much younger than when I had seen them last."

This will unfold in a surrounding that is sheer delight.

As the mysteries of your life unfold, you may see the "wall" of eternity scroll down. All can be brought before you in an instant. You will delight in what you overcame!

Kindness brings joy and somewhere in your mysterious mission is the task to love despite circumstances.

Every hardship will be "gold."

A smile on earth reflects the sunshine of Heaven.

"The weather was absolutely perfect in terms of temperature and humidity," said a blind man who saw the surroundings. "It was so fresh, so unbelievably fresh that mountain air on earth could not even come close. It was absolutely refreshing, wonderfully refreshing."

"It seemed to be all-encompassing," said another blind man named Brad. "It seemed like everything, even the grass I had been stepping on, seemed to soak in that light. It seemed like the light could actually penetrate through everything that was there, even the leaves on the trees. There was no shade; there was no need for shade."

The light shimmers; it causes warmth (as if you are inside of it).

There are jasper and gem stones—the blind have described such also, just like anyone else who goes through the experience.

Yet they are not gems—not like stones of the earth.

There may be a wall. There may be a bridge. We will meet *ancestors*. We will map our genealogies. Families bear purpose and you will learn that purpose. When Kimberly Sharp died, the way she described the feeling of eternity was with words she used as a child: "homey home." It is more than home. It is our origin. Our spirits were created here. They were infused into our bodies when the Lord knitted us in the womb. Before we existed, He knew us, says the Bible. Gabrielle Keller testifies that "it was everything you could wish for if you were trying to imagine Heaven. The feeling of wonder and peace that I had was something I have never experienced before or since. A group of people met me, walking up to me with their arms outstretched. I had never seen any of them before, but somehow they were familiar."

How quickly it passes! We are here for but 29,000 days. The clock ticks. We are "homeward bound." And this is what we must bind ourselves to: our true home.

Not forgiving will stifle you.

It is a lesson of the Crucifixion: to forgive no matter what, to release to the Father, and endure pain without purveying it. *Christ gave us the keys to eternity* on Calvary. We can rise like Him—not resurrect, bodily (that was for the Son of God), but to rise above the antagonisms, the hurts, of this passing world.

Fear? Pain?

There was the woman who was diagnosed with basal cell carcinoma on her nose and though this is not a deadly illness, "I was in the deepest state of depression and despair that I have ever known. Two nights before surgery I was sleeping when I was awakened by a bright light shining in my eyes. I opened my eyes to see a large sphere of light floating about five feet in front of me. There was a light within it that was rotating from left to right. This sphere spoke to me: 'You aren't afraid, are you?' Seeing this light made me fearless. In fact I was filled with the most incredible peace I have ever known. Suddenly the light went through me. It didn't reflect off of me or anything like that. It went straight through me. As it did, I was filled with unconditional love which was so complete and powerful that I would need to invent new words to describe it.

"I asked that my cancer would be removed. I prayed actually. And the light said that what we think of as prayer is [sometimes] more like complaining and we are frequently begging to be punished for something that we are simply going to do again in the future.

"He asked me to think of my own worst enemy and I did. Then he said to send all of my light to my worst enemy. I did and a sudden burst of light went out of me and returned as if it had been reflected back from a mirror. I became aware of every cell in my body. I could see every cell in my body. It was the sound and sight of light coming from my being. I was crying, laughing, shaking, trying to hold still and trying to catch my breath. When I finally recovered, the being of light said, 'now you have prayed for the first time in your life.'"

17

Final Bliss

We take the good from any mystical event and leave the rest. It says this in the New Testament [*1 Thessalonians* 5:19]. We test the spirits [*I John* 4:1]. The brush with death often transforms the person into a mystic of sorts and there are events reported on the deathbed that match the mysticism of famous persons such as St. Padre Pio. There is also deception. There are suspect near-death episodes. There are many spiritual teachings that seem illuminated but have a troubling undercurrent. One enormously popular "course" about miracles originated with a woman who later denounced the inspiration on her deathbed (she claimed to be hearing the Voice of Jesus) and suffered what one priest described as a "black hole of depression."

Behind the "light" can be the shining dark.

And so we are careful that all fits with Scripture and is backed by the sacraments.

We must be covered with the Precious Blood of Jesus—which both protects and sanctifies.

The truth is known when the conscience is clear and the conscience is made clear when we go to Confession. It is very important to avail ourselves of what Christ left us when He told us to eat His body and drink His blood. This is unity with Him *before* we actually see His light.

Yet we must keep an open mind in a world that is so often mysterious.

Did not John try to grant us a preview in *Revelation*:

"Immediately I was in the Spirit; and behold, a throne was standing in Heaven, and One sitting on the throne. And He who was sitting was like a jasper stone and a sardius in appearance; and there was a rainbow around the throne, like an emerald in appearance. Around the throne were twenty-four thrones; and upon the thrones I saw twenty-four elders sitting, clothed in white garments, and golden crowns on their heads."

That is the height!
We enter at the countryside.
We need to be forgiving to enter.
Total forgiveness.
Be kind to someone every day and do it out of love.
This will get you there.

"Just as we crested the top of the hill, I heard my father's voice calling, 'Jesus, Jesus, Jesus,'" remembered a woman named Betty Malz. "His voice was a long distance away. I thought about turning back to find him. I did not because I knew my destination was ahead. We walked along in silence save for the whisper of a gentle breeze ruffling the white, sheer garments of the angel. We came upon a magnificent, silver structure. It was like a palace except there were no towers. As we walked toward it, I heard voices. They were melodious, harmonious, blending in chorus and I heard the word, 'Jesus.'"

While the angel walked, said Betty, she had the feeling that they could go wherever they willed themselves to go. Movement was instant.

"The angel stepped forward and put the palm of his hand upon a gate which I had not noticed before," she wrote. "About twelve feet high, the gate was a solid sheet of pearl, with no handles and some lovely scroll work at the top of its Gothic structure. The pearl was translucent so that I could almost, but not quite, see inside. When the angel stepped forward, pressing his palm on the gate, an opening appeared in the center of the pearl panel and slowly widened and deepened as though the translucent material was dissolving.

"Inside I saw what appeared to be a street of golden color with an overlay of glass or water. The yellow light that appeared was dazzling. There is no way to describe it. I saw no figure, yet I was conscious of a Person. Suddenly I knew that the Light was Jesus, the Person was Jesus."

There is Ian McCormick, who nearly died when he was stung by a toxic jellyfish while diving for lobster on the island of Mauritius.

"I couldn't believe it, but as I stood there a radiant beam of light shone through the darkness and immediately began to lift me upward," said Ian, once a non-believer, now a convert. "I found myself being translated up into an incredibly brilliant beam of pure white light—it seemed to be emanating from a circular opening far above me. I felt like a speck of dust being drawn up into a beam of sunlight. This light wasn't just physical, but was giving off a living emotion. Halfway down was another wave of light—this time it gave off pure peace—followed by another wave: of pure joy.

"Coming out of the end of this tunnel, I found myself standing in the Presence of awesome light and power—it seemed as though even the constellations in the universe must find their energy source from this focal point.

"Words appeared in front of me," added Ian. "'God is light and in Him is no darkness at all (*1 John* 1:5).' I had never read a Bible before in my life so I didn't know this was straight out of the scriptures. God is light, I thought, is pure light—I see no darkness here, I have just come from darkness—I see no evil, no shadows—this is pure light—am I standing in the presence of God?"

It was Jesus.

When we concentrate on the Light we get the Light. And so we hear from so many: that they are led to Jesus or even by Him to the place that is really home as home could never be—a place all the joys of earthly life are but the flash of a second, a drop in the ocean. The way there is often both similar and different—designed to the individual and a metaphor in many cases for the state of the soul. Varied countrysides. Beautiful arbored paths. Pope Gregory the Great recorded near-death cases back in the sixth century including that of a man who had died of the plague.

"He was drawn out of his body and lay lifeless, but he soon returned and described what befell him," wrote the great pontiff in what may be the first detailed near-death accounts. "At that time there were many people experiencing these things. He said that there was a bridge, under which ran a black, gloomy river which breathed forth an intolerably foul-smelling vapor. But across the bridge there were delightful meadows carpeted with green grass and sweet-smelling flowers. The meadows seemed to be meeting places for people clothed in white. Such a pleasant odor filled the air that the sweet smell by itself was enough to satisfy the inhabitants who were strolling there. In that place each one had his own separate dwelling, filled with magnificent light. A house of amazing capacity was being constructed there, apparently out of golden bricks, but he could not find out for whom it might be."

There are the gorgeous valley floors, the foothills, the endless highlands; no prairies; no deserts; a wide and lofty place—the crown of the world, and then higher; large fields of grass—gold grass; blue flowers, flowers on two-foot-stems, goldenrods; fantastic animals (but no mosquitoes); a pergola of vines; numerous birds; huge butterflies; animals not of the earth; new forms of life.

All share in beauty.

"The tremendous love experienced in the afterlife is like having the love of every mother in the universe pour into us for all eternity," wrote researcher Kevin Williams.

"If I lived a billion years more, in my body or yours, there's not a single experience on earth that could ever be as good as being dead," said a woman named Dianne Morrissey, if we recall.

"I saw the most beautiful lakes," said still another modern testimony. "Everything was white. The most beautiful flowers. Nobody on earth ever saw the beautiful flowers that I saw there. I don't believe there is a color on this earth that wasn't included in that color situation that I saw. Angels were floating around like seagulls."

Angels as cherubs. Angels as warriors—rushing to a mission.

Angels responding to prayers that are beams of light.

Ask your angel every morning to guide you to the best preparation.

"The trees, shrubs, and flowers were perfect," is another account. "They had no dried leaves anywhere. Even trodding on vegetation did not damage it. It was not only the beauty of individual flowers that impressed, but the way they were arranged in the gardens and how they complemented each other in color and size."

"Time didn't seem to matter," said another we must quote. "I felt like I had all the time in the world just to stroll down the lane and enjoy the feeling of peace and serenity."

And that ethereal atmosphere is preparation for still greater, higher realities!

The longer one travels, it is said—Dr. Lundahl and Dr. Widdison mentioned—the more impressive become the surroundings.

"Those who die go to different states or places and do not see each other at all times," said a girl named Daisy Dryden who "died" as a child, "but all the good are in the state of the blest."

If there are many ways of existing in hell and purgatory, so too are there the many levels of Heaven and we can surmise that the Blessed Mother is at the very top. She is in the highest reaches. In Georgia, an unusual image appeared on the future grave of a woman. It was taken to be an angel (this was a Baptist cemetery). It looked very much, too, like the Blessed Mother.

One man from Louisiana wrote to me about a severe heart attack—so severe that doctors had to induce a coma. When they did, his organs shut down. He was given no chance of survival. "I was awakened not in this world," he said, "but face to face with Our Lady who told me it was not my time to come."

Where she is, where Christ is, are too the highest orders of angels.

How many orders?

We could not know. But we will.

"Small flower-lined paths led up to individual homes and the houses seem to be small and occupied by individual family members," said Lundahl and Widdison. Or families occupy whole areas. A celestial picnic?

Some see trees with "fruit," others vast forests of oaks and elms and trees that are unfamiliar to earthly eyes—all towering and symmetrical and accenting the light.

There is the countryside but then, dramatically, there may be what seems like a city—or a series of "cities." This is where some have seen the place of life review. It is where others have seen what seemed like vast libraries—so vast as to be "endless" (like all the buildings in Washington together, in the words of one). Dr. Ritchie described the library he saw as "the size of the whole University of Richmond," where he gazed into rooms lined floor to ceiling with documents "on parchment, clay, leather, metal, paper." The thought came to him (as to others who have seen a similar place) that "the important books of the universe" were assembled here. During his experience the psychiatrist entered another "building" that seemed to have a hushed atmosphere and he was startled to see people in a passageway. "I could not tell if they were men or women, old or young, for all were covered from head to foot in loose-flowing hooded cloaks which made me think vaguely of monks," he wrote in *Return from Tomorrow*. "But the atmosphere of the place was not at all as I imagined a monastery. It was more like some tremendous study center, humming with the excitement of great discovery. Everyone we passed in the wide halls and on the curving staircases seemed caught up in some all-engrossing activity; not many words were exchanged among them. And yet I sensed no unfriendliness between these beings, rather an aloofness of total concentration. Whatever else these people might be, they appeared utterly and supremely self-forgetful—absorbed in some vast purpose beyond themselves. Through open doors I glimpsed enormous rooms filled with complex equipment. In several of the rooms hooded figures bent over intricate charts and diagrams, or sat at the controls of elaborate consoles flickering with lights. I'd prided myself a little on the beginnings of a scientific education; at the university I had majored in chemistry, minored in biology, studied physics and calculus. But if these were scientific activities of some kind, they were so far beyond anything I knew, that I couldn't even guess what field they were. Somehow I felt that some vast experiment was being pursued, perhaps dozens and dozens of such experiments."

We discern. Heaven or a realm below it?

"The eyes of faith permit us to see that the heavenly and earthly cities interpenetrate and are intrinsically ordered to one another, inasmuch as they both belong to God the Father, who is 'above all and through all and in all,'" Pope Benedict XVI told a pontifical academy.

Others have viewed souls busy with tasks that could not be determined. "I felt just wonderful," said a woman whose death occurred in 1960. "I felt no pain. I felt like an observer, floating there between two worlds, one that I knew well and one that I didn't know existed. In time it seemed as though the ceiling was paved with blue-white clouds, and the air seemed sprinkled with gold dust. It became very bright."

"I remember walking in a garden filled with large flowers," said a woman who had her experience as a child.

Said James Beck, who had an experience way back in the 1860s, there was "an angel standing just above my head where I lay—defending the house. Standing upright with a drawn sword in his right hand extended above his head and his face lifted up to Heaven facing due east. He was tall and stood very erect. He was clothed in a complete suit of armor with a helmet cap or covering upon his head. It appeared and shone like pure silver. I saw plainly the joints at the knees and arms."

Another saw "these beautiful beings" who "sang the most lovely and extraordinary music I had ever heard. They were identical, each equally beautiful. When their song was over, one of their number came forward to greet me. He was exquisite."

Angels, concluded Lundahl and Widdison, "seem to be those beings who carry on the day-to-day operations of the City of Light and serve as messengers from the spirit world to those still on earth. They serve as escorts-guides for those who have died, and they serve as guardians for individuals on earth. When emergency situations warrant it, warrior angels have been known to protect those who need protection. Angels have the physical appearance of humans, with the major exception that they glow. They are beings of light—not reflected light, but light that comes from within. This is felt as pure love, complete peace, and total acceptance."

There are many kinds of angelic beings.

There are many realms.

We will all know one day.

Up there, we will see angels.

Up there, we will be exploring.

Up there, we will be learning.

Up there, we will view the entire scheme of our family histories.

Up there, we will adore.

Up there, we will intercede.

Up there, we will build.

Up there, we will invent.

Up there, we will approach work with no anxiety nor system of finance nor taxes nor worry.

Everything is already taken care of.

We have no needs.

The vastness of God will take eternity to investigate, to comprehend, to appreciate (if ever that is possible). It will unfold in a way that will startle even the most imaginative astronomer.

Let God be at the center of your thoughts. Yearn for Him. Love Him intently. Nothing is more important than loving God.

Do that and there will no fear (whatsoever). At the transition, the words "Jesus, Jesus, Jesus" must be on your lips.

The splendor!

Unlike our own, the buildings in Heaven do not reflect light so much as exude it. They are a source or at least they direct it. This is why there are terms like a "city of light."

"It was similar to cities on earth in that there were buildings and paths, but the buildings and paths appeared to be built of materials which we consider precious on earth," was the detailed testimony by a woman named Amelia. "They looked like marble, and gold, and silver, and other bright materials, only they were different. The buildings and streets seemed to have a sheen and to glow."

The walls are to keep those who are not ready out, to protect those who are at work in this sacred place. Or so it is said. There is a demarcation. There are the homes that range from very small to huge (proportionate to one's spiritual progress), and it is said that they are not complete until one's mission on earth is accomplished.

Our greatest basilicas, our temples, and our cathedrals—our towers—are attempts to capture what the intuition anticipates.

"White crystallized marble." "Translucent stone." "Buildings with no floors or ceilings." "Windows with no panes." There are, too, the "living waters" that flow through what one woman, Marietta Davis, described as "marble channels or through beds of golden sands, while others rose to lofty heights and then flowed into glowing streams or sprouted from a sea of fountains in the city. In the countryside, it may be a pond or lake with waters that heal the spirit and exude a melody, acting alive."

Architecture is created in a way we have not yet conceived, in this first "city," and then, far off, is another city, if we can accept some accounts.

Here, it is said, everything not only emanates light but is formed by it.

One man claimed he was taken "to the next kingdom which so exceeded the first in beauty and glory that I was again amazed and requested permission to stay. I cannot command language to describe the beauty of the inhabitants and scenery."

Next came a third kingdom which was far more beautiful in glory and order than the former two: so pure and white that he was overwhelmed with joy (but not allowed to enter).

"These accounts are typical of all accounts, in which every feature of the City of Light seems to blend together harmoniously, perfectly, and beautifully, with the flowers, shrubs, and trees complementing the physical structure of the buildings," wrote Lundahl and Widdison. "The cities of light are just that: they are very bright and literally emanate light. No sun or extra source of light is needed or apparent. There are no areas of darkness. The cities appear to be filled with beautiful gardens, flowers, shrubs, and trees that perfectly complement their physical structures of walls, gates, streets, houses, and various buildings with their magnificent interiors and furniture. There are several cities built of light on different levels, and each appears to have a greater grandeur than the last one. Those who can't tolerate the light of a particular city are not found there. All of these cities are so superior to any on earth that it is indescribable. There is intercity travel that seems relatively free from higher to lower realms, but restricted from lower to higher realms."

According to the researchers, those who have glimpsed the upper reaches described specific buildings or areas that were guarded. "Reasons for limiting access, both stated and implied, include the protection of individuals from being exposed to environments they could not withstand; to keep people from disrupting the work of those already in the city; to protect sacred areas from people who do not or cannot appreciate them; and to keep people out of areas in which they do not need to be or are not qualified to enter," claimed Widdison and Lundahl, who taught at Northern Arizona University and Western New Mexico University (respectively) and penned a book called *The Eternal Journey*.

One realm unfolds into another. The farther we venture into eternity, the more magnificent. Those in Heaven—the majority of deceased we have known—probably have not begun yet to grasp an idea of how much it will continue to unfold. *Such is its extent.* In those cities, many describe the inhabitants as peaceful, joyful, but also busy—preoccupied with what they have been assigned.

Mysterious errands.

And yet also, still, in the afterlife, the basic unit is the family.

Family is very important. There is reunification. There is reconciliation, as everyone now understands what the others went through: what burdened them, why they acted as they did, what was true and what was a misconception. We will love without condition.

No jealousy.

No pettiness.

No possessiveness.

You will come face to face with those who were family members as well as guardians.

"My guardian angel was dressed in a pure white robe and seemed kind of transparent," testified another. "I noticed my body was very different as on earth. It lacked nothing, no pain or limitations, just perfect. I became particularly interested in the robe I was wearing. I glowed and my whole body seemed to emit light that made me also kind of transparent. There were countless people there, all dressed in white robes; some were walking in the garden. Others were flying through the air at incredible speed. All around was just happiness in its purest form.

"Suddenly, I thought of some people back on earth that died during my childhood. They were all in our church. I thought that if what we teach there back on earth is true then they should all be here in Heaven. I was thinking of a lady who was incredibly happy on earth, and I was certain that she should be around here. Out of the blue before I could finish my thought there she was walking past me, only ten times happier. I just thought of the particular person and right there they appear in front of me. Then I became so amazingly joyful because they are all here safe and sound and seemed incredibly happy."

The idea we will encounter fantastic light in the company of a guide parallels an account taken from no less than Venerable Bede, the famous English monk who was born in the seventh century and recorded the account of "a man already dead" who "returned to bodily life and related many notable things that he had seen, some of which I have thought valuable to mention in brief." The holy monk then went on to quote the man, who lived in the country of the Northumbrians, as saying: "A handsome man in a shining robe was my guide, and we walked in silence in what appeared to be a northeasterly direction. As we traveled onward, we came to a very broad and deep valley of infinite length. He soon brought me out of darkness into an atmosphere of clear light, and as he led me forward in bright light, I saw before us a tremendous wall which seemed to be of infinite length and height in all directions.

"As I could see no gate, window, or entrance in it, I began to wonder why we went up to the wall. But when we reached it, all at once—I know not by what means—we were on top of it. Within lay a very broad and pleasant meadow. Such was the light flooding all this place that it seemed greater than the brightness of daylight or of the sun's rays at noon."

The "guide" then told this man: "You must now return to your body and live among men once more; but, if you will weigh your actions with greater care and study to keep your words and ways virtuous and simple, then you will win a home among these happy spirits you see."

In 1583, a young prince named Paolo Massimo was dying. He had been visited daily by Father Philip, founder of the Oratorians and one of the greatest religious figures of Rome (later Philip Neri). On March 16, we see in an account, the priest was delayed and by the time he arrived, Paolo was dead. According to the testimony of the child's father, the priest began to pray at the side of the bed with his hand on the boy's forehead. After seven or eight minutes of intense prayer he sprinkled the youth with Holy Water and called his name. Paolo opened his eyes. The boy spent several minutes talking with the holy priest, but then explained that he would rather go to Heaven to join his mother and sister. Hugging Father Philip one last time, Paolo fell back on the cushions and died.

St. Faustina also was given visions of Heaven and hell. Of paradise she wrote: "Today I was in Heaven in spirit, and I saw its inconceivable beauties and the happiness that awaits us after death. I saw how all creatures give ceaseless praise and glory to God. I saw how great is happiness in God, which spreads to all creatures making them happy; and then all the glory and praise which springs from this happiness returns to its source; and they enter into the depths of God, contemplating the inner life of God, the Father, the Son, and the Holy

Spirit, whom they will never comprehend or fathom. This source of happiness is unchanging in its essence, but is always new, gushing forth happiness for all creatures."

One day young St. Catherine of Siena had been sent with her brother Stephen to the house of their married sister Bonaventura, states a biographical note on her. As they passed the fountain of Fontebranda, Catherine, who was looking up at the Church of St. Dominic, which stands on the opposite hill, "saw in the heavens the figure of Our Lord robed and crowned: He stretched out His right Hand and blessed her solemnly with a smile of sweetness. Catherine stood rooted to the ground, oblivious to the things around her, with her eyes fixed to the beautiful vision. Stephen turned to look for her. 'Catherine,' he cried, but she did not come. 'Catherine, Catherine!' he repeated, running to his little sister and pulling her by the hand, saying, 'What are you doing? Why do you look up like that?' In response Catherine burst into tears because the vision was gone. 'Ah,' she said, 'if you had seen what I saw you would never have pulled me away,' but she did not tell her brother what had happened. It was not for several years, when it had become a habitual thing for her to see and converse with Our Lord, that she told her confessor of this early vision."

After this foretaste of Paradise, we are told, St. Catherine became more reserved and thoughtful. She had witnessed the Lord in His beauty, and He had drawn her pure heart to him forever. Shortly after, she made a vow to the Holy Mother consecrating herself to God. "Here I give my faith and promise to Him and to thee that I will never take another spouse but Him, and so far as in me lies, will keep myself pure and unspotted for Him alone to the end of my days."

18

Into the Heart of God

Most important is the encounter with Jesus.

In the afterlife, we will know with utter certainty that He was precisely Who He said He was.

No matter what someone believes, he or she must encounter Him.

There is no other way to the final place of "rest"; there is no paradise without Him; those who don't know Him here will encounter Him in the hereafter.

We know that not only from the Bible but due to what so many near-death experiencers—Christian or non-Christian—have said.

Yes, there are some who don't see Him. Yes, there are Hindus and Buddhists who see Buddha or their "gods."

Is this Heaven allowing the environment to conform to beliefs, forging it in a familiar way (or is such a vision a deception)?

We attempt to discern. We know only that even atheists have seen Jesus.

He told one man that he should never worry if people doubted his story or could not understand what he was

157

telling them because "one day everyone will come to see for themselves what you have seen."

Said Eadie: "It was the most unconditional love I have ever felt, and as I saw His arms open to receive me I went to Him and received His complete embrace. I felt His enormous Spirit and knew that I had always been a part of Him, that in reality I had never been away from Him. I knew that He was aware of all my sins and faults, but that they didn't matter right now. He just wanted to hold me and share His love with me, and I wanted to share mine with Him. There was no questioning who He was. I knew that He was my Savior, and friend, and God. He was Jesus Christ, Who had always loved me."

"Everything that I had been told [by angels] was consistent with the Bible and particularly with the Gospel stories of Jesus Christ," added that art professor I have quoted, who said that after his experience "I would read a passage from the Bible and shout to my family, 'This is exactly what they were teaching me!' I thought I had discovered the greatest book in the world. Every word spoke to me on a deep personal level. The Bible resonated with the truth as I had been given it. Through His brief life with us, we know nothing can separate us from the Love of God. Nothing we do can separate us from God unless we want this. No matter what we have said or done, God is willing, eager, and begging us to turn back to God. Even if we think we have nailed God to a tree, God looks into our eyes and says, 'I forgive you because you do not know what you are doing.'"

Thus, yearn for God. Want Him more than anything. Dedicate your life to making others feel good. That will get you there.

A heart of love is the Heart of God.

The greatest emotion, far and away, is joy—not fear, not judgment.

The vast majority completely lose their fear of death.

No matter what they have done, or how they feel about themselves, Jesus is there to love them.

"The love and warmth which emanate from this Being to the dying person are utterly beyond words—and he feels completely surrounded by it and taken up in it, completely at ease and accepted in the Presence of this Being," said Dr. Moody. "He senses an irresistible magnetic attraction to this light. He is ineluctably drawn to it."

"I looked around the garden, and there was this Being," said the woman who, as a child, had a near-death encounter. "The garden was extraordinarily beautiful, but everything paled in His presence. I felt completely loved and completely nourished by Him. It was the most delightful feeling I've ever known. I can still feel that feeling."

"I don't remember going up a tunnel or anything like that, but I was transported into a very peaceful situation, a place that looked like a very white and bright light," said a woman known as "patient 44" in a study by Dr. Morse—a woman who at the age of fifteen was struck by lightning. "In our everyday experience you would have to squint because you couldn't even look at it. But I could look at it in the state I was in and it was very peaceful. To describe it in our language is very difficult. It was like being in an airplane over clouds during sunset. But instead, the wavy clouds and the red glow were all around me so I could touch it. The feeling that went with it was utter and total peace. It was a peace I had never really known before or since."

"I was eight years old when I almost drowned in a swimming pool," said another. "I remember a deep black void. Then suddenly there was a bright light and I felt a strong sense of peace."

"Seeing the light made me fearless," testified a woman who saw it while in a state of depression. "In fact, I was filled with *the most incredible peace* I have ever known.

Whoever was speaking to me knew what all my problems and fears were. All of my burdens slipped away. Suddenly the light went through me. It didn't reflect off of me or anything like that. *It went straight through me.* As it did, I was filled with unconditional love which was so complete and powerful that I would need to invent new words to describe it."

"I stared in astonishment as the brightness increased, coming from nowhere, seeming to shine everywhere at once," said the psychiatrist, Dr. Ritchie.

"It was impossibly bright."

"Brighter than hundreds of suns."

"There was light all around Him."

"It was unspeakable. I didn't want to come back. Once I came into His Presence, I felt I had come to the ultimate point in my life."

"I know that while it was indescribably brilliant, it wasn't just light."

"This was a living being, a luminous being approximately eight-feet tall and surrounded by an oval radiance."

"His love was greater than all human love together."

"His love totally enveloped me."

"He was indescribably wonderful: goodness, power, knowledge, and love. Ever since I have joy in my heart!"

"I saw that the light immediately around Him was golden, as if His whole Body had a golden halo around it, and I could see that the golden halo burst out from around Him and spread into a brilliant, magnificent whiteness."

It was a "pure crystal light, not any kind of light you can describe on earth."

"All loving."

"All forgiving."

"As I reached the source of the light, I could see in. I cannot begin to describe in human terms the feelings I have over what I saw. It was a giant infinite world of calm, and love, and energy, and beauty."

"It is not a radiance which dazzles, but a soft whiteness and an infused radiance which, without wearying the eyes, causes them the greatest delight, nor are they wearied by the brightness which they see in seeing this Divine beauty," wrote the great mystic, St. Teresa of Avila. "So different from any earthly light is the brightness and light now revealed to the eyes that, by comparison with it, the brightness of our sun seems quite dim and we should never want to open our eyes again for the purpose of seeing it. It is as if we were to look at a very clear stream, in a bed of crystals, reflecting the sun's rays. It is a light which never gives place to night, and being always light, is disturbed by nothing."

This is Jesus. He is there just as He said: the Light of the world—and of eternity. He's at the right Hand of the Father. He is the Master not just of our world, but all others.

We can have His Light now and blend with that Light even before death such that it will surround us when we make the transition. Oh glory in this! *We step into the eternity we have fashioned.* We step into the state of our souls. Keep heading for the Light, noted one man, and your shadow will fall behind you.

Dedicate your life to making others feel better. This will get you there. During the Rosary, ask to see hidden faults. Correct them. If there are knots in your life, ask the Blessed Mother, the saints, to untie them. Know that you must find a purpose in life, that there is a rationale behind everything that happens, that you should not be a slave to time (which one day will seem so trivial to you), that some of the "greatest" or "worst" or "monumental" events in your life are no big deals (in the context of eternity); that you should not be formed or dominated by the thoughts of others. Fear not pain and surely not death, which will be a release into His Arms. Except for basic sustenance, forget the material. Be open to what the Lord sends you, to what life holds for you, and do not compare it to that of others. Assisting people is what counts in life. Don't trouble yourself trying to outdo others; forsake competition; enjoy life as it unfolds and when it ends.

We take to Heaven the love we have built within and it brings us to the level that corresponds with it.

Your spirit will be comfortable at the place in eternity that reflects it.

"I am not going to think poorly of anyone," you should vow right now, while there is such a chance at direct heavenly entry. Even if we need to correct others, we also must say, "I love you just as you are." "I am going to think gently of everyone." "It is important for each person to succeed, as we are all part of the Creation." "We are all connected." *View everything you think or say or do as if you are watching it*, which you will some day. What have I done to make the world a better place? What have I done for others that was not the least bit selfish? Where do I have habits and obsessions? Am I thankful? Am I just going to church—or letting the Eucharist enter and transform me (as the Light of Christ)?

Have I glorified Him in everything?

Only in prayer after a devout life with the intercession of saints and those angels and reception of the Eucharist that brings the Light of Jesus right within us are we safe to pursue the destiny. It is the narrow gate. With prayer—with Scripture ready in our minds, on our tongues—do we discern the "light." What a light the real One is!

Accept only those spirits who confess Jesus, Son of God.

Ignore not evil but focus on the positive.

Let His Blood be your shield.

Remain in His embrace. Stay in His Light. You will not feel the passage.

Remain in His embrace.

Pray for this every day.

In a flash, you will see His true essence. It will astonish you. This is guaranteed. Your fondest hopes for what may lie ahead will be exceeded. Your love will unfold like a red carpet on a stairway. Rid yourself of all resentment. Resent no one. Laugh off slights. Care not if you are loved in return. *True love expects nothing.* It needs no compensation. True love loves for the sake of love. It perfects. So, we should perfect everything. Trust beyond trust. Surrender beyond abandonment. Every morning, ask God for the *gift of compassion*. Find balance. Only balanced souls make it directly to Heaven. You will know by joy. We go as we are. We step into the mirror of our souls. *Let me be an instrument of Your love.* This Jesus will love to hear you say. It draws Him like a magnet. So does gratitude. It makes us healthy here (and forever). Gratitude, with love, balances us (like a fine Swiss watch). Find the big in the small. Glory in every chore of life. Each is wonderful!

Each is a ticket.

Hope beyond hope. Release all pride. Persevere beyond endurance.

God will not let you fall.

Become a living representation of the Eucharist.

Void yourself *of* self.

Humility is your shield.

Hearken not to thrills but to the joy in the depths (and heights) of the Spirit.

Smile upon all with kindness. Kindness points your mouth and eyes and spirit upward! In the Eucharist, let Jesus come into you that you may transmit Him to others.

Live each moment to the fullest.

Let every deed be what you would like to be remembered by.

Harden never your heart.

Here is where we feel Him! God is love. Love is light. God is the Light of life that loves.

God is everything.

Beyond any place is the final merging with Him.

"Bliss beyond words," said a former non-believer.

"What I felt was this enormous peace and instantaneous heavenly knowing," said Paul Palnik, who was teaching art at the University of Arkansas when his episode happened. "I remember thinking, if this is Heaven, I want to go. I want to be absorbed into this light—brighter than bright, lighter than light, more alive than life. It is impossible to describe—almost like a liquid light, like a billowing, living light in the blackest black floating in space."

Incredible. Beyond brilliant.

"Greater than all human love put together," goodness, power, and wisdom that transcends human conceptions—a glory that is "blinding" without blinding—overwhelming without making one uncomfortable; far better than expected.

There will be tears of joy when first you lay eyes on Him.

He will hold you close; He will stroke you; He will heal you—of everything.

With Him, you will traverse impossible distances.

He will be your Father, your brother, your cousin, your best friend.

Joy will billow through you. It will always be a summer breeze.

"This was the most totally male Being I had ever met," wrote the psychiatrist, who heard a voice say that he was in the Presence of the Son. "If this was *the* Son of God, then His Name was Jesus. This Person was power itself, older than time and yet more modern than anyone I had ever met. Above all, I knew that this Man loved me. Far more even than power, what emanated from this Presence was unconditional love. A love beyond my wildest imagining. This love knew every unlovable thing about me —the quarrels with my stepmother, my explosive temper, the sex thoughts I could never control, every mean, selfish thought and action since the day I was born—and accepted and loved me just the same."

"I knew—I don't know how I knew, but I knew—I had to go to that light, that there was safety in that light," said a devout Catholic woman from Louisiana with whom I spoke years ago. "I went into the light and it was brilliant and the light was Christ, and He looked just like He did when He ascended into Heaven. He wore the white tunic and He had His Hands up. I saw the wounds. He embraced me—and the love! I have never known that kind of love. I thought I knew what love was. Being a mother I love my children and grandchildren so much, but the love of Christ is so consuming, it's just unbelievable."

We meld quickest with that Light by being light here on earth.

Get rid of all that focuses only on you and you will be taking a great step into luminosity.

The light! The endless, powerful Light! It forms Him. It holds us. It takes us into a new realm that will open unto other realms. It washes away every hurt—every single negative in our lives. It purifies. It makes joy our air. It teaches us that death is not to be feared, that life continues, that every event in our lives happens for a reason, that love is completely more important that anything material.

It teaches us what it says in the Bible.

Above everything: work at how you treat people. The whole world is not worth a single harsh word. Act as if all of Heaven is watching. It is. Your every good act is cheered. You are totally understood. If you love Jesus, you are not condemned.

You will never be alone.

All hail the glory that awaits!
All hail the goodness to which we aspire.
All hail the attempts at purity.
The angels.
The Blessed Mother—Queen of Heaven!
All hail the glory of a faith where we receive Him even before death!
The love that perfects.
Perfection.
His Light.
His Peace.
His Love.
All hail! All praise!
All sing hallelujah now and forever with those we have known and loved and to whom we will return—never to part from them again.

Notes

Many books, personal conversations, interviews, internet searches, and e-mails went into this work, mainly books. Research into "near-death" episodes can be traced back to Plato, the account from Paul in *2 Corinthians* 12:2, and then in more detail to Pope Gregory the Great, as documented in *Other World Journeys* by Carol Zaleski (Oxford University Press, 1987). The accounts from Gregory originate in the Pope's classic work, *Dialogues*, from the Sixth Century. See also Venerable Bede's report on a near-death vision in *Ecclesiastical History of the English People* (from the eighth century). The modern-day seminal work was Dr. Raymond Moody's *Life After Life* (1975), which coined the term "near-death experience" and was followed by his *Reflections on Life After Life* and *The Light Beyond*. For deathbed visions see *At the Hour of Death*, by Dr. Karlis Osis and Dr. Erlendur Haraldsson. The lessons of near-death experiencers are from Dr. Kenneth Ring's excellent and highly-recommended book, *Lessons from the Light*. RaNelle Wallace's book is *The Burning Within*, used for descriptions of Heaven and its colors and flowers and also the life review among other aspects. Another seminal book for descriptions of the afterlife is *The Eternal Journey* by Craig Lundahl and Harold Widdison. The most detailed near-death experience and one I also draw from is

Betty Eadie's *Embraced by the Light*. She is referred to at several junctures (described as a Seattle resident or the woman with the extensive near-death experience). Angie Fenimore's account is from her book, *Beyond the Darkness*. The quotes from seers who encountered the Blessed Mother at an apparition site are from Jan Connell's *Visions of the Children*. Another quote on afterlife encounters is from Dr. Carla Wills-Brandon's *One Last Hug Before I Go*. The account on the woman watching in the operating theater is in *Death's Door* by Jean Ritchie. The quote from Kimberly Clark Sharp is in her book, *After the Light*. Grace Bubulka's and Christ Taylor's quotes are from accounts on www.near-death.com. The quotes from Elane Durham are in *Echoes from Eternity* by Arvis S. Gibson. For life reviews I also used *What Tom Sawyer Learned from Dying* by Sidney Saylor Farr; *The Near-Death Experience: Mysticism or Madness* by Judith Creesy; *Glimpses of Life Beyond Death* by Tony Bushby (responsible for several quotes on the review); *Echoes from Eternity* (previously cited); *Return from Tomorrow* by Dr. George Ritchie; *Transformed by the Light* by Dr. Melvin Morse; *Nothing Better Than Dying* by Kevin R. Williams, whose book is also used for additional characteristics, including the relationship of light to love; and *My Descent into Death* by Howard Storm. The quote from the blind person is from *Mindsight*, by Dr. Ring (see above) and Sharon Cooper. The quote from Gabrielle Keller is in *Death's Door* (cited previously). The quote on the woman with skin cancer is from *Transformed by the Light* by Dr. Melvin Morse. Betty Malz's remembrance is in her book, *My Glimpse of Eternity*. The quote from Paul Palnik is from *The Journey Home* by Philip L. Berman. The quote on energy affecting the health is from the International Association for Near-Death Studies, or IANDS. Used as general background or for specific quotes, also: *The Case for Heaven* by Mally Cox-Chapman; *Glimpses of Heaven* by Trudy Harris; *90 Minutes in Heaven* by Don Piper with Cecil Murphey; *Ordered to Return* by Dr. George Ritchie; and *Life of the World to Come* by Carol Zaleski. The description of the tunnel at the beginning of the book is from *Fast Lane To*

Heaven by Ned Dougherty. See too: *Visions of God* by Ken R. Vincent; *The Place We Call Home* by Robert J. Grant; *On Life After Death* by Elisabeth Kubler-Ross; *Beyond Death's Door* by Dr. Maurice Rawlings; *Beyond This Reality* by Grace Bubulka; *Light and Death* by Dr. Michael Sabom; *The Truth in the Light* by Dr. Peter Fenwick; *Life at Death*, another book by Dr. Ring (who added vast seminal material, in the style of Dr. Moody); and *Life Beyond Death* by Tony Bushby. The description of demons is from *23 Minutes in Hell* by Bill Wiese. Choo Thomas' account is from her book, *Heaven Is So Real!* The vision of St. Catherine of Siena comes from a book by Mother Frances A. Forbes (*St. Catherine of Siena*). Many books were used in researching this work, books by sincere people and often medical professionals although often I do not subscribe to their religious views or perspectives, which often stray into psychic or New Age realms. Caution and prayer are greatly advised, as there is deception here as there is among alleged apparitions. As with all such books, I often recommend discernment, for the near-death field can even head into realms of reincarnation or mediumistic phenomena, which I find highly inadvisable (along with any other means of "communicating" with the dead). In following Scripture, we test the spirits, and take what is good, and leave the rest; no spirit that does not confess Jesus as Savior is legitimate. Any that take us away from Christianity are at least partially suspect. See also *An Unpublished Manuscript on Purgatory* (available at www.spiritdaily.com) and *After Life*, which I wrote in 1997.

About the author

A former investigative reporter, Michael H. Brown is the author of more than twenty books, most of them Catholic. He has appeared on numerous TV and radio shows, and contributed to publications from *Reader's Digest* to *The Atlantic Monthly*. He is the author of the Catholic bestsellers *The Final Hour* and *After Life* and lives in Palm Coast, Florida, with wife Lisa and three children. He is also director of the Catholic news website, Spirit Daily (www.spiritdaily.com).

Special thanks to Judy Berlinski, Lisa Brown, and Kathleen Jenkins for editorial assistance; and thanks to Pete Massari for the cover design.

Other books by Michael H. Brown

Available at www.spiritdaily.com

AFTER LIFE (Heaven, Hell, and Purgatory)

TOWER OF LIGHT (current prophecy)

THE GOD OF MIRACLES (real cases of answered prayers)

SENT TO EARTH: God and the Return of Ancient Disasters

SEVEN DAYS WITH MARY (devotional prayers)

SECRETS OF THE EUCHARIST

THE FINAL HOUR (the Blessed Mother's apparitions)